The Royal United Services Institute Whitehall P[illegible]

Trade, Development a[illegible] Africa

All Sides of the Same Coin?

Report of the 2005 Tswalu Dialogue

Edited by Terence McNamee, Greg Mills, Monde Muyangwa and Kurt Shillinger

www.rusi.org

CO-PRODUCED BY:

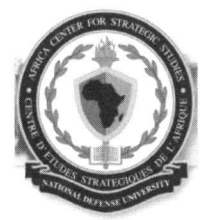

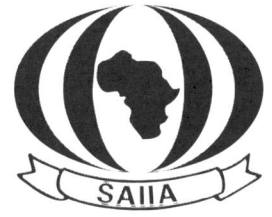

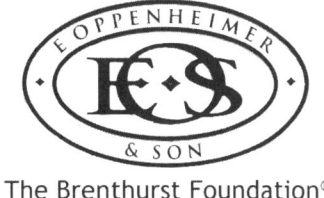

The Brenthurst Foundation®

First Published 2005
© The Royal United Services Institute for Defence and Security Studies

All rights reserved. No part of this publication may be reproduced, stored in a retrieval system, or transmitted in any form or by any means, electronic, mechanical, photocopying, recording or otherwise, without prior permission of the Royal United Services Institute.

Whitehall Paper Series

ISBN 0-85516-112-4
ISSN 0268-1307

Series Editor: Dr Terence McNamee
Assistant Editor: Klaus Dalgaard

Whitehall Papers are available as part of a membership package, or individually at £8.00 plus p&p (£1.00 in the UK/£2.00 overseas). Orders should be sent to the Membership Administrator, RUSI Membership Office, South Park Road, Macclesfield, SK11 6SH, United Kingdom and cheques made payable to RUSI. Orders can also be made by quoting credit card details via email to: membership@rusi.org

For more details, visit our website: www.rusi.org

Printed in Great Britain by Stephen Austin & Sons Ltd. for the Royal United Services Institute, Whitehall, London, SW1A 2ET UK

RUSI is a Registered Charity (No. 210639)

Contents

Preface   v

Introduction and Acknowledgements   vii
Greg Mills and *Kurt Shillinger*

1. **THE GLOBAL ENVIRONMENT**   1
   Advancing Freedom, Peace and Prosperity in Africa: Statement by the United States Assistant Secretary of State for African Affairs   *Jendayi Frazer*   3
   What the External Community can do for Africa: Assessing the Report of the Commission for Africa   *Richard Dowden*   9
   Africa and the Global Environment: Is there a dramatic opportunity to change things?   *John Battersby*   15
   African Stand-by Forces   *Andrew Stewart*   23
   Africa's Challenges as Global Challenges, and the Viability of Nepad to Address Them   *Shannon Field*   29
   The Changing Security Environment   *Christopher Coker*   35

2. **TRADE OBSTACLES AND PROSPECTS FOR GROWTH**   45
   Trade, Development and International Institutions: 2005 and Beyond   *Razeen Sally*   47
   The WTO and FTAs – An East Asian Perspective   *Barry Desker*   57
   Trade Obstacles and Prospects for Growth   *Paraschand Hurry*   63
   Promoting African Trade: Issues, Prospects and Challenges   *Mills Soko*   71
   The Future for Regional Integration in sub-Saharan Africa   *Richard Gibb*   79

3. **'GOODS' AND 'BADS': OBSTACLES FOR AFRICAN STABILITY AND SECURITY** 87

Governance in sub-Saharan Africa: Building the Foundation for Prosperity and Security   *Jeffrey Herbst*   89

The Obstacles to Stability and Security in Africa   *Seth Obeng*   99

Development as a Strategic Concern: Re-orienting the Response to Faltering States   *Kurt Shillinger*   105

Health, Wealth, Terrorism and Energy: A Portent of Western Security Dilemmas in Africa   *Greg Mills*   113

Appendix   123

Biographies   129

Preface

The 2005 Tswalu Dialogue was held roughly two months before the opening of the G8 summit in Gleneagles, Scotland on 6 July 2005.

When Tony Blair established the Commission for Africa a year earlier, one of its aims was to use the United Kingdom's Presidency of the Gleneagles summit as a platform for its work. Naturally, many of the participants at Tswalu – mindful that Africa would be top of the upcoming summit's agenda – speculated on the likely commitments to Africa – and their impact – that G8 leaders would agree to at Gleneagles. What follows is a brief summary of the key commitments and goals they signed up to, extracted from the final communiqué of the summit. For readers, it should serve as a useful reference for assessing the findings and conclusions of the individual papers, which were written prior to Gleneagles.

Critically, the focus now shifts to delivery – of the G8 commitments to Africa, and African leadership to their own people and donors. This collection of papers from Tswalu focuses on the commitments, conditions and capacity necessary for such delivery – of stability, security and development – to occur.

At Gleneagles, several African nations joined the G8 discussion on Africa and development, including the leaders of Algeria, Ethiopia, Ghana, Nigeria, Senegal, South Africa and Tanzania. So too did the heads of the African Union Commission, International Monetary Fund, United Nations and the World Bank. Discussion centred on how to accelerate progress towards the Millennium Development Goals – especially in Africa, which has the furthest to go to achieve these targets by 2015. African leaders set out their personal commitment to drive forward plans to reduce poverty and promote economic growth; deepen transparency and good governance; strengthen democratic institutions and processes; show zero tolerance for corruption; remove all obstacles to intra-African trade; and bring about lasting peace and security across the continent. The G8 in return agreed a comprehensive plan to support Africa's progress.

The G8 agreed:
- To provide extra resources for Africa's peacekeeping forces so that they can better deter, prevent and resolve conflicts in Africa.
- To give enhanced support for greater democracy, effective governance and transparency, and to help fight corruption and return stolen assets.
- To boost investment in health and education, and to take action to combat HIV/AIDS, malaria, TB and other killer diseases.

Preface

- To stimulate growth, to improve the investment climate and to make trade work for Africa, including by helping to build Africa's capacity to trade and working to mobilize the extra investment in infrastructure which is needed for business.

The G8 leaders pledged to back this plan with substantial extra resources for countries which have strong national development plans and are committed to good governance, democracy and transparency. Realizing that poor countries must decide and lead their own development strategies and economic policies, the G8 agreed that aid for Africa should be doubled by 2010 (aid for all developing countries will increase, according to the OECD, by around $50bn per year by 2010, of which at least $25bn extra per year for Africa).

The summit also agreed that the World Bank should have a leading role in supporting the partnership between the G8, other donors and Africa, helping to ensure that additional assistance is effectively co-ordinated; and that all of the debts owed by eligible heavily indebted poor countries to IDA, the International Monetary Fund and the African Development Fund should be cancelled, as set out in the Finance Ministers agreement on 11 June. The G8 welcomed the Paris Club decision to write off around $17 billion of Nigeria's debt. The G8 and African leaders agreed that if implemented these measures and the others set out in the comprehensive plan could:

- Double the size of Africa's economy and trade by 2015.
- Deliver increased domestic and foreign investment.
- Lift tens of millions of people out of poverty every year.
- Save millions of lives a year.
- Get all children into primary school.
- Deliver free basic health care and primary education for all.
- Provide as close as possible to universal access to treatment for AIDS by 2010.
- Generate employment and other opportunities for young people.
- Bring about an end to conflict in Africa.

Introduction and Acknowledgements

Greg Mills and Kurt Shillinger*

The 2005 Tswalu Dialogue: Ten Points of Discussion

- The impact of China's and India's economic growth and increasing investment and trade adventurism in Africa, especially on the continent's extractive and manufacturing sectors. The rise of these Asian giants poses both important opportunities and severe challenges for Africa.
- Africa's increasing diversity in terms of successful states and those which have failed. How should the international community respond to this widening disparity? Should it rescue those at the bottom or focus on moving the middle tier of states upward? Are the relatively successful states able, entitled or willing to speak for the failures?
- The viability of institutions to ensure African security, notably the African Standby Force. While African policy in this regard is laudable, the human and financial resource reality make these long-term projects. Means have to be found to encourage such longer-term goals while at the same time dealing with more immediate needs and realities.
- Scepticism about the value of international trade regimes in delivering African trade growth, including the impact of a reduction of agricultural subsidies. At the very least, African states will require strong national institutions in order to take advantage of the growing, dynamic, but extremely challenging international market.
- Tension between attempts to establish bilateral free trade agreements and the multilateral trade regime through the World Trade Organization.
- The dominance of protectionist constituencies on the continent. Africa's demands for unilateral trade concessions from the industrialized countries ignores the advantages of freer trade for African countries, including reducing tariffs on exporters and barriers to cheaper imports.

---

* Christopher Clapham, Jeffrey Herbst, Terence McNamee and Peter Draper also contributed to this introduction.

- The poor record of aid expenditure in Africa. What might positively change this record? The utility of aid has become especially important given calls by the Africa Commission and others to massively increase concessional flows to countries south of the Sahara.
- The impact of new oil investments in Africa – anticipated to be more than US$100 billion during the next decade. Might this fuel become a set of new competitive tensions around both governance and between investing states, notably China and the United States?
- The likelihood of the acceptance and success of the recommendations of the Africa Commission and the impact of relative failure/success in this regard.
- The role of human and resource flows between Africa and the rest of the world. Stemming the 'brain drain' is crucial if Africa is to integrate with the international economy and address critical domestic problems, including the HIV/Aids pandemic. Remittances from the Diaspora are one of the few resource flows to Africa that is seemingly guaranteed to grow.

Over the past five decades, Africa has been the recipient of more than US$500 billion in foreign aid. Today, however, the average person on the continent is poorer than in 1970; faces a rapidly shortening life expectancy from the spread of malaria, TB and HIV/Aids; and is even more likely to grow up illiterate. The continent receives less than 1 per cent of global foreign direct investment, is more vulnerable than any other to the economic aftershocks of international conflict such as escalating oil prices, and has the greatest concentration of weak, failing and collapsed states.

But Africa is also higher on the international agenda than at any previous time in history, for both economic and strategic reasons. In January the United Nations released an exhaustive report outlining the obstacles to Africa's progress toward reaching the poverty reduction targets of the Millennium Development Goals and proposing a range of possible solutions. Two months later, British Prime Minister Tony Blair unveiled the findings and recommendations of the Commission on Africa, which brought influential partners from the North and Africa to develop a blueprint for Africa's economic recovery. The continent's problems were also due to feature prominently at the G8 summit in Gleneagles, Scotland in June, and be a predominant concern for the European Union during the second half of the year.

Against this backdrop, the fourth **Tswalu Dialogue** considered the imperative for Africa of the three increasingly braided strands of global diplomacy: trade, development and security.

The Tswalu Dialogue, an annual event launched jointly in 2002 by hosts Jennifer and Jonathan Oppenheimer and the South African Institute of International Affairs (SAIIA), provides a unique forum for political leaders, diplomats, senior military strategists, business people, policy analysts and academics to discuss matters of critical importance to Africa's development. The opportunities presented to Africa in the twenty-first century are as great as the challenges it faces, and it is thus a key objective of the Dialogue to promote creative new thinking by growing a network of the most influential people from across the broadest range of constituencies.

In previous rounds, the Dialogue considered the heterogeneous nature of the performance of African states; the challenges to development and security posed by the continent's 'big states' such as Nigeria, Sudan, Angola, the Democratic Republic of Congo and Ethiopia; the consequences for Africa of the wars in Afghanistan and Iraq; prospects for Africa's signature development initiative – the New Partnership for Africa's Development (Nepad); and the positive and negative consequences of globalization on peace and security, democracy and development in Africa.

Since 2004, the Dialogue has enjoyed the generous support and participation of the Ford Foundation and the Konrad Adenauer Stiftung. The same year, the London-based Royal United Services Institute for Defence and Security Studies (RUSI) became an organizing partner. This year the Dialogue grew again, adding the US-based Africa Center for Strategic Studies and The Brenthurst Foundation, a new South African think tank devoted to the study of African economic growth.

Like last year, the focus of the Dialogue was paved by the preparation of a formal research agenda in the form of pre-circulated research papers, which provided the foundation for the various discussion sessions. **The Tswalu Dialogue** *is held according to 'RUSI rules'. Consequently, beyond the arguments presented in the prepared papers, which follow this introduction, attributions are withheld from the conference report.*

A full list of participants and the programme of events is attached to this summary.

Thursday 28 April 2005

In the traditional address following the opening dinner, **Jendayi Frazer,** (then) **US Ambassador to South Africa**, discussed Washington's approach to promoting peace and development in Africa. She emphasized three main 'bottom-lines':

First, US policy toward Africa rests on a belief that Africa's future must fundamentally be shaped from within. Consequently, Washington seeks to support key lead states and sub-regional organizations to improve Africa's capacity to uplift itself. It identifies countries for strategic engagement on the basis of diplomatic influence and economic and military strengths. These key partners, accordingly, are Nigeria, Kenya, South Africa and Ethiopia. The US also targets smaller democracies that are pursuing economic reforms, including Mozambique, Botswana, Benin, Ghana and Mali. Through the Millennium Challenge Account (MCA), Washington has tied US$5 billion in development assistance to performance, even though there is today only one African country (Madagascar) which has benefited from this initiative.

Second, the US commitment to peace and security is 'unquestionable and unassailable' even though Washington was 'not going to have an Africa policy that was rhetorically pleasing'. During its first term, the current Bush administration's top priority was stopping conflict in five key states: Sudan, the Democratic Republic of the Congo, Burundi, Sierra Leone/Liberia and Angola. Now, in the second term, it has shifted from preventing mass killing to achieving 'stabilization through democratization' by promoting democracy in those places where the US has the strategic capacity to affect meaningful change. The ambassador specifically ruled out Somalia in this context, but identified Zimbabwe and Côte d'Ivoire as well as the role of the Lord's Resistance Army in northern Uganda.

Frazer stressed the importance of avoiding 'arbitrary targets' for development, and noted that, contrary to popular belief at the time, the intervention to topple Saddam Hussein's regime in Iraq had not left Africa neglected. She placed special emphasis on building institutional capacity and combating the three main health threats – malaria, tuberculosis and HIV/Aids – and on combating terrorism through the US$20 million Pan-Sahel and US$100 million East Africa Counter Terrorism initiatives. Stability also requires greater opportunities for trade, increased private investment and an end to agricultural subsidies. She reiterated that Washington alone has proposed 100 per cent cancellation of debt stock among Heavily Indebted Poor Countries (HIPC). In the trade domain, the US African Growth and Opportunity Act (AGOA) has affected 6,400 tariff lines, resulting in the creation of 190,000 new jobs in Africa. AGOA has spurred a 65 per cent growth in US-Africa trade since its inception, amounting to US$44 billion currently, half of which is a direct result of the Act.

Third, Africa and the world have an historic window of opportunity to address the continent's persistent problems. There is broad international consensus on the measures required: institutional transformation of the WTO; the ending of agricultural subsidies; and debt relief. Only the finer points need agreement. Critically, Ambassador Frazer argued, Africa must take responsibility to engage proactively with willing external partners to ensure sustained economic development.

Friday 29 April 2005
Session One: The Global Environment
In assessing the nature and imperatives of the current global security environment, this session took note of three sets of questions:
1. *Will there be a new international trade regime that is more favourable to African countries? Will the specific problems of agricultural subsidies be addressed?*
2. *What resources will the international community provide to promote peace in Africa? Will the international community now depend on African leaders – as in Côte d'Ivoire – to negotiate compromises while maintaining a detached attitude? Has the African demand for peacekeepers exhausted the supply?*
3. *How will international efforts to fight terrorism affect African countries? Does the war on terror provide specific opportunities for African countries?*

The central theme emerging from the preparatory papers for this session is global interdependence. We live in a world where threats and the responses to them require realistic dialogue both within and across hemispheres.

In his preparatory paper, however, **Christopher Coker**, urged caution. First, what is meant by security today? In a world divided into premodern, modern and post-modern states, there is no common understanding of security. The global discourse on security is shaped disproportionately by Western anxiety. How might different perceptions and priorities be bridged? Second, there has been a huge shift in both the role of and perceptions about states. States are no longer the sole determinants of security, and citizens no longer have confidence in the ability of their governments to protect them. As Coker expressed it, 'The nation-state is in crisis'. Put differently, states are no longer 'structurally fit' to provide security on their own. Hence the growth in public-private partnerships seen, for example, in Iraq, where private security firms are playing an unprecedented role in post-war reconstruction. This sharing of sovereignty is a sharing of security, and it makes all concerned uncomfortable. Third, there is no single paradigm through which to understand the world and its imperatives. There has been a transformation in the language of security: The West acts on assessments of risk while the developing world is concerned with threats.

Moving from the theoretical to the practical, **John Battersby**, **Andrew Stewart** and **Shannon Field** sought to identify in their papers the practical requirements of meeting the goals of Nepad, the UK Commission on Africa and the African Standby Force. Battersby highlighted the ongoing need to counter negative perceptions about Africa. In drawing the link between security and development, Field made the case for greater Western commitment to countering corruption, stemming the flow of arms to Africa and transforming the economic environment through debt cancellation, increased aid and trade reforms. Stewart, meanwhile, argued that security, economics and governance are the 'three-legged stool' of African stability and development. There is little chance of creating a viable African reaction force by 2010, as is currently desired. Rather, this must be seen as a 30-year project requiring assisting African countries to address the three 'legs' at the continental, regional and national levels. There is a need to replace competition between African states and between Western states with collaboration among African and Western partners to achieve both top-down and bottom-up approaches to building a deployable African security force. Bilateral engagement is probably the easiest and first means for developing this logistical, political and tactical capacity state by state.

The discussion that followed began with a pointed question: What is Nepad for? Its achievements thus far have been modest at best. Even so, there was a general consensus that an African plan for continental development – which Nepad is – was both necessary and desirable. Although still in its formative stages, Nepad should therefore be supported. One critical challenge on its agenda that was repeatedly emphasized was what African countries can do to encourage the repatriation of human and financial capital back to the continent. The stripping of skilled human capital – by countries like the UK and Canada, who are involved in sophisticated recruiting drives aimed at, for instance, South African health providers – was seen as a major problem. Even more worrying was the continued failure of African countries to attract foreign direct investment. Perception remains a key problem: African countries have done little to present a picture of stability or create an environment conducive to inward investment. Trade negotiations were also identified as an area where reform is essential to correct the severe imbalances that hinder African development. It was argued the poor performance of African companies is at least in part due to the approach African governments take to negotiating trade deals. Northern states enter talks with offensive positions on behalf of their commercial sectors, whereas African governments typically pursue agreements based on political objectives. It is critical to develop capacity and a dialogue between African trade negotiators and the businesses they represent.

The rising chorus of initiatives for doubling aid to Africa prompted debate about the merits of different forms of development assistance. Intrinsic to aid arrangements are conditions sometimes driven by unrelated political agendas of donors. One alternative is human resource development (the example of the Asian countries was cited), which unlike aid, would enable African countries to choose their own course. But views differed on the extent to which aid should be de-emphasized as a means to African development. Further disagreement centred on (what one discussant argued was) the tendency of African leaders to participate widely in regional and international fora and frame domestic issues and problems in a regional or international context. Should African leaders instead redouble their efforts on creating specific, unique solutions to their domestic problems? Not exclusively. Without South Africa's persistent intervention in Burundi, it was argued, there would have been no progress toward peace in the Great Lakes region.

Another area of debate related to security values. Is African regionalization undermining the influence and strength of the nation-state? Is increased regionalization in Africa a sign of the 'state' reinventing itself in order to survive? Deprived of any transcendental function, are states now merely about the business of management and the maintenance of power?

What is the most effective means of foreign co-operation with African armed forces and the criteria for deployment of international troops in Africa's theatres of conflict? It was argued that a clear objective and sufficient political will are pre-conditions for external military peace-keeping. It was also noted that although multilateralism in military matters is often essential politically, it presents serious problems operationally. Britain's highly successful bilateral military co-operation with Ghana was cited as a prime example of why bilateralism, specifically where it draws on an existing historical relationship, is the ideal arrangement, with the European partner acting as mentor and assisting with major logistics while the recipient African country provides the basic force requirements, food, logistics, equipment and so forth. It was noted that central to the success of the Ghana-UK relationship is that the equipment used by Ghanaian forces is entirely local. Overall, while the 'big three' – France, Britain and the US – have a vital mentoring role to play in Africa's regional security arrangements, Africa must take the lead.

Session Two: 'Goods' and 'Bads': Obstacles for African Stability and Security
This session responded to the following questions:
1. Does Africa have the potential to improve governance to take advantage of more international trade and aid concessions? Which African countries/regions have the greatest hopes of dramatic forward progress?
2. Will the tempo of conflict in Africa continue to decline or are some countries at risk of new or renewed violence?
3. There are some African countries that have such poor environmental circumstances or that are so ravaged by conflict that development in the near term is not a real possibility. What can the international community do to improve their prospects?

As **Jeffrey Herbst** noted in his preparatory paper, there is a convergence in understanding among African and industrialized countries about the importance of governance to development, but there is no consensus on the condition of governance in Africa. The Columbia University economist Jeffrey Sachs, for example, argues that governance in Africa is generally fine, while the UK Africa Commission argues it is not. The US government, meanwhile, takes a middle view, targeting engagement only toward those developing states that reach prescribed levels of performance. Herbst argues that governance can be objectively measured through a variety of factors, including per capita income, how long it takes to negotiate a contract and the potential for grievance mediation. The total African population, he noted, is concentrated in countries with poor governance according to these indices. As Zimbabwe shows, meanwhile, poor governance can lead to dramatic decline, whereas nation building takes a long time. Africa is marked by three broad conditions of governance: the well-governed, such as South Africa and Botswana; the post-conflict or conflict ridden states, such as Angola and the Democratic Republic of the Congo; and those in the middle of these extremes, including Mozambique and Ghana, where the potential exists for creative engagement. Herbst indicated three primary remedies for poor governance: routinization of elections; exemplary treatment of corruption; and improved protection of property rights. What is missing in the global discourse, however, is a clear contribution from Africa about what governance means, which needs to be forged through societal consensus.

Ashraf Gamal El-Din, meanwhile, provided a case study of

Egyptian economic reforms during the past two decades to underscore the importance of trade and investment to both domestic and regional stability. He noted that whereas intra-Asian trade amounted to US$650 billion in 2000 and intra-European trade US$1,625 billion, trade among African states totalled just US$11 billion. The obstacles to trade within Africa include poor infrastructure, lack of access to capital, weak banking, credit and insurance facilities, and a lack of information. The creation and conduct of business is hobbled by too many regulatory constraints, including high corporate taxation and burdensome labour laws. In Egypt, he noted, it takes 4.2 years to close a business. El-Din identified a range of necessary measures to introduce greater competition and accelerate privatization. He also underscored the importance of making stock markets work more efficiently, boosting education systems both for existing and future working forces and encouraging the growth of SMEs (small and medium-sized enterprises) through subsidies and incubators.

Seth Obeng drew the link between state performance and economic, political, environmental and state security. Poor governance, he noted, results in inadequate resources for development, rising expectations of restive populations, negative external influences and political intolerance. Legitimacy of government is critical to establishing internal stability. This implies and requires, as Herbst also noted, institutionalized regular transition in governance. It also necessitates stronger constitutionalism, including adoption of a bill of rights, term limits for state leaders, judicial independence and creation of structures for mediation and reconciliation. Establishing security in Africa also depends on curbing negative foreign interference such as arms sales.

The sudden flurry of reports offering solutions to Africa's development crisis symbolizes, importantly, a new world concern for conditions on the world's poorest continent. But, as **Michael Spicer** argued, there is an urgent need for rapid movement toward microeconomic reforms. Positive trends on the continent include: the spread of market economics; acceptance of the link between good governance and growth; and the spread of South African business activity across the continent. On the negative side, the increased interest in oil is likely to encourage corruption in the weakest states, while other factors – irrational state borders, halting economic liberalization and insufficient domestic investment – undermine development and deepen negative perceptions about Africa. Transparency initiatives are welcome, as is greater knowledge sharing among companies doing business in Africa. But success will hinge on the political will to pursue long-term, internally driven solutions.

The discussion started by downplaying the role of regional organizations in improving governance in the continent. There has been a long and generally dispiriting experience of such organizations, which have tended to distract leaders from the generally more important task of improving domestic governance and engaging in the pressing domestic issues that are essential to resolve. There are salutary lessons to be learned from experiences of governance failure, among which that of Côte d'Ivoire has been especially traumatic. Critical factors here were the lack of any mechanism for assuring succession to the founding leader, Felix Houphouet-Boigny, who stayed in power much too long and stifled alternative political leadership. Exactly the same problem has occurred in nearby Togo, where the difficulties have been revealed by the death of President Gnassingbe Eyadema. 'Term limits' are a vital factor in improving the standard of governance. Further factors inhibiting good governance were over-dependence on external support – in this case, from France – and problems of political identification and exclusion, which reserved political power to representatives of one part of the country – the south in Côte d'Ivoire, the north in Togo. The peculiar land-tenure system was a further factor leading to conflict in Côte d'Ivoire. Where, on the other hand, it had been possible to maintain a high degree of national cohesion even during difficult times, as in Ghana, it was possible to learn from previous failures and improve levels of governance once political conditions permitted. Even though elections do not always deliver democracy, as this would be understood in the West, peacefully contested elections nonetheless helped to sustain political stability and confidence. Some notably successful African states, such as Botswana, had never experienced an opposition victory, but retained viable political systems.

The discussion also emphasized the need to discriminate between African states, and to replace one-size-fits-all formulae with solutions that differentiate between more and less successful states. In this respect, the approach adopted by the MCA, with its measurable and broadly objective criteria for allocating aid, were generally to be preferred to the approach of either the Africa Commission or Jeffrey Sachs. African states still tend to be guided too heavily by the norms of continental solidarity inherited from the liberation era – a factor that may inhibit the revelation of problems – and differences during the African Peer Review Mechanism.

Some problems are essentially policy related and can be tackled by governments prepared to address them, especially by challenging anti-development internal vested interests. Key factors in improving the business environment include over-regulation, poor or contradictory investment policies and obstructive labour market regulations. Broader problems relate to social risk, which in a country such as Nigeria are such that a 25 per cent annual return on investment is needed just to break even. Risk may also be reduced by effective measures to ensure the separation of the military from politics, and in turn of politics from the military. While FDI is a key indicator of the creation of an effective governance framework, this is actually dependent on domestic investment: Prospective investors are sensitive to the actions of indigenous businessmen, who may be expected to understand local conditions better than they do, and cannot be expected to invest so long as domestic capital is expatriated.

Among African regions, the greatest prospects of dramatic progress were in southern Africa, where these were aided by the presence of an economically successful regional power, extensive South African investment and a generally shared set of economic and political assumptions. Even so, the continuing deterioration of Zimbabwe dampens optimism and badly affects external confidence.

There was a broad consensus that levels of conflict in Africa had peaked, but that new or renewed violence could not be excluded. A particular danger in this respect, given its importance to the continent as a whole and especially to West Africa, was the potential for violence and governance breakdown in Nigeria. Other regions, including the Guinea-Sierra Leone-Liberia-Côte d'Ivoire zone, central Africa and the Horn, retained a high risk of further conflict. In such cases, the ability of the international community to restore order and create the conditions for development are extremely limited. While 'fire brigade' operations as in Sierra Leone and Côte d'Ivoire may be successful in halting or reducing violence in the short term, rebuilding public confidence necessarily requires a successful domestic political process that is difficult, if not impossible, to provide from outside.

Session Three: Trade Obstacles and Prospects for Growth
This session posed the following questions:
1. *What is the likely mix of foreign investment, aid and domestic savings that African countries will have to depend upon to promote growth?*
2. *What do African countries have to do to actually take advantage of decreases in agricultural subsidies?*
3. *Will growth patterns across the continent continue to diverge? What is the impact of an increasingly heterogeneous Africa for regional organizations?*
4. *Will African countries be able to develop indigenous economic plans that they can explain to their publics?*
5. *What are the prospects for poverty reduction in the near future?*

Razeen Sally argues that there are increasing limits to progress on liberalization at the WTO and through regional free trade agreements. Rather, the main thrust will come through unilateral liberalization, led by China particularly but now also India. Regarding the WTO, Sally notes that decision-making processes have been fundamentally transformed as the membership has expanded, leading to its 'UN-ization'. This has been matched by the coverage and depth of negotiations, now no longer confined to border barriers (tariffs and quotas) but extending into intrusive areas of domestic governance. He noted that this does not mean the Doha round will fail; rather, that it requires refocusing on market access and streamlined decision-making procedures.

What, then, are the prospects for African participation in the World trading system? Sally argues that preferential trading schemes have many problems, characterized by weak rules and asymmetrical deals favouring northern partners. More seriously, they distract governments from what they should be doing at home. The spat of new international initiatives for Africa's development, he concludes, make good news on trade but are wrong on aid.

Barry Desker notes that the shift to bilateralism in East Asia was presaged by the slowdown in WTO negotiations combined with the shift in developed countries, especially the EU, to regulation-intensive negotiating platforms. These trends alarmed East Asian governments, which preferred to 'do what is possible, rather than what is desirable'. Furthermore, because FTAs can be negotiated faster than broader WTO initiatives, they are less vulnerable to shifting sentiments resulting from national political cycles. Desker argues that developing countries should focus on trade facilitation and build the institutions commensurate with managing while liberalizing trade flows. He notes that developing countries have greater tariff protection than developed countries while privileging imports from developed countries at the expense of those from developing countries. This undermines south-south trade, and these problems are compounded by tariff escalation practiced by developed countries on developing country exports.

Finally, **Paraschand Hurry** argues that the full gains of trade liberalization would accrue to countries if supported by policies affecting the macroeconomic environment, domestic markets, quality of institutions, infrastructure and successful engagement in the international economy.

Discussion began with the utility of the theory of comparative advantage and free trade in a world of mobile capital. It was noted that if the WTO is sidelined in favour of preferential FTAs, comparative advantage would be threatened and resource allocation distorted. Furthermore, it was suggested that the degree of mobility of capital is overstated. China and India's success is fundamentally a story of comparative advantage. It was agreed that FTAs need to be carefully calibrated, and that pursuing this route could undermine the WTO and threaten a return to the undemocratic decision-making that characterized the Uruguay round.

Regarding unilateral liberalization, it was noted that there are serious problems with structural adjustment policies in the African context. It was agreed that such liberalization processes have to be domestically driven rather than externally induced. The former has been the East Asian and now South Asian route, whereas the latter has characterized Africa's path. Furthermore, it was noted that liberalization has to be consistent and properly managed through appropriate sequencing.

In the **Friday evening post-dinner talk** and again on Saturday afternoon, **Michael Power** explored the impact of China's rise on geo-economics generally and Africa specifically.

The essential story is that sometime around 1999 China seems to have reached its tipping point in terms of its industrialization and what was an already impressive growth rate went into overdrive. From 1999 to 2003, for example, China jumped from the fourth largest to the largest global producer of computers, reflecting a 446 per cent increase in growth. This phase of industrialization is extremely resource intensive as China moves into its capital intensive stage of growth. For a smaller country, this sort of take-off would not be sufficient to override the cyclical pattern typical to resources. But in the case of China – which is now the flagship of the Asian fleet – the size of the engagement is so huge that it cannot help but create a 'super cycle' in resources, bumping them up to a higher price plane. This does not mean the end of cyclicality for resources – just the 'temporary' suspension of it. That said, China's take-off, Power argued, will run at high speed for a decade yet, so 'temporary' should be interpreted to mean 'short'.

For Africa, this is by and large good news as a high percentage of its exports are resource-based. The result is that a millennium old trade route across the Indian Ocean is being revived. But China is not simply importing Africa's output; it is actively investing in Africa to find new deposits – particularly of oil. The most obvious example of the latter is in Sudan, where Chinese investment has underwritten the development of a new industry, paying not just for the production facilities but also for a 1,000-mile-long pipeline as well. Elsewhere in the continent, Chinese investment in Zambian copper and Angolan and West African oil has been recorded. More – much more – is expected.

But China's take-off is not all good news. Two negative consequences in particular need to be noted. The first is that many nations in Africa – by allowing the resource price windfall to strengthen their exchange rates – risk giving themselves a bad case of the Dutch Disease. The second – which is a symptom of that Dutch Disease – is that Africa's industrial middle risks being hollowed out as domestic production is undermined by cheaper, more competitive imports and exports (sometimes including even Resource Exports – think South African gold) are constrained by an uncompetitive exchange rate. In January 2005 alone, imports of Chinese textiles to the US rose by 75 per cent following the expiration of 30-year-old global textile quotas, a convulsion that holds immediate and potentially devastating consequences for cloth weaving factories across Africa and the developing world. What makes China different to most other trading partners is that they are both the cause of the benefits arising (via their voracious appetite for resources) as well as the cause of its negative side effects (via its export of all things manufactured thereby undermining Africa's industrial heartlands).

Saturday 30 April 2005
The morning sessions were divided into two breakaway groups.

Group One: Trade
Mills Soko, **Gui-xuan Liang** and **Richard Gibb** made initial presentations on prospects for African trade. The discussion that followed was rich and nuanced, leading to a general consensus on the important tasks that confronted African countries if they hoped to promote trade. In particular, the group focused on five points:
1. **A strong state is required if countries were to trade more.** A strong state is not necessarily a large state, but one that makes productive investments in infrastructure and human capital and that provides a secure environment for investors. A state without properly working institutions cannot grow through trade; indeed, African leaders may mistakenly devote too much of their energies to regional and international trade negotiations and not enough to the critical task of fostering their own national institutions. A strong state also has some capabilities to reduce the number of losers when adjusting to international trade negotiations and to ameliorate their absolute loss.
2. **The comparative advantage of African countries must be**

understood. Right now, the comparative advantage of most African countries is in raw material production; indeed, most countries export only a very few commodities. In contrast, the comparative advantage of large African countries is in cheap labour. That suggests complementarities in international trade but also challenges because Asian countries right now have close to a stranglehold on what had traditionally been the first rungs of industrialization. However, comparative advantage is not static: countries can take steps to diversify their comparative advantage and seek out niches not currently exploited by the international economy.

3. **China is a threat and an opportunity for African countries.** China's phenomenal rate of growth will increase the demand for most African commodities. That should lead to an up-tick in short-term African growth rates. However, African countries will then face the profound challenge of how to funnel the increased revenue streams from exports to productive uses such as increased investment in infrastructure and education. The record of resource-dependent countries worldwide using increased export revenue streams productively is poor. Oil is notable for how often the opportunities provided have been squandered but the record of other commodities is not encouraging. Those African countries that manage the resource booms or boomlets will do well while others may simply enrich some elites while the majority of their populations remains impoverished.

    China insists on the sovereign prerogatives of national governments. This is appealing to African governments but may sabotage international efforts to promote good governance in resources producers, especially oil. The Chinese approach is also potentially in tension with the African Peer Review Mechanism. China's commitment to securing oil supplies in Sudan has also obstructed international efforts to end the genocide in Darfur.

4. **Regional and international trade negotiations are important for African governments but must be understood.** Most regional integration efforts in Africa have failed to deliver, in part because states are weak and the integration efforts are too heavily dependent on donors. Regional integration cannot substitute for important national efforts at institutional development. Even if regional integration is successful soon, current inter-African trade is so low that gains will be limited. The Southern African Customs Union is one of the few regional integration successes. It is highly dependent on a regional

hegemon. It was not clear if other regional hegemons are necessary or sufficient for regional integration efforts to succeed.

International trade negotiation efforts are also important for Africa. There was scepticism about who speaks for Africa. Especially important for a highly diverse continent, the G20 group that includes large developing countries cannot necessarily represent all poor countries. International trade negotiations also have to figure out ways to compensate losers. Finally, it was noted that there is considerable uncertainty about how much the proposed liberalization of agriculture trade will help African exporters (because of pessimism about their supply response and competition from other countries) and how badly net food importers would actually be hurt.

5. **Finally, rising flows of remittances from the African Diaspora are a major source of 'export' earnings for African countries.** These remittances flow directly to individuals and help to reduce poverty. Reducing transaction costs associated with remittances would be extremely helpful. Some African countries may also seek to capture remittance flows to enhance public revenue.

Group Two: Stability and Security

Monde Muyangwa, **Kurt Shillinger** and **Greg Mills** presented views on three core security issues, respectively: methods of building security partnerships between the West and Africa; the threats posed by weak states and what to do about them; and the prospects and challenges of broader, 'human' security concerns, notably around health, poverty and governance. All three papers emphasized the interdependence between stability and development.

Five inter-related issues dominated the ensuing discussion:

1. **The need for incrementalism**, focusing on 'the art of the possible', using limited Western aid budgets to 'reinforce success', avoiding grand schemes and grandstanding. Capacity building was crucial for service delivery, and acknowledging limitations in the former meant not attempting to do everything at once in the latter regard.
2. **The importance of managing the downside risks** – notably poor governance – of increased investment in the oil sector in Africa. China's economic growth offered an opportunity for both African resources and for African-based businesses in the Chinese market. But there were downsides that needed to be managed, including the impact of cheap Chinese products flooding African markets and displacing African manufacturers; and, if Sudan was anything to go by,

the impact on attempts to promote transparency and good governance norms in its burgeoning investments in the Africa oil sector.
3. **The record of oil producers in Africa** had, until now, been exceptionally poor in terms of improving living and governance standards. Means had to be found to support the Extractive Industry Transparency Initiative especially through the AU and the UN, and lessons needed to be learned from the positive role of industry players in the Kimberley Process in regulating the diamond trade.
4. **Sound leadership committed to popular welfare** was a *sine qua non* for African prosperity and stability, as it had been in East Asia's success. The cultivation and education of the next generation of African leadership, both civilian and military, was crucial, and incremental strategies had to be found in this respect.
5. **New ideas and all strategies needed to be considered in securing Africa**. The discourse on development needed to move beyond one based on hemispheric divides and conditionalities to one of consensus among developed and developing states on threats and risks, thereby enabling a broader range of international responses to the crises of faltering states free of the political interests of individual external actors.

In the lunchtime keynote talk, **Richard Dowden** explored options for constructive external engagement with Africa, following on the findings of the UK Commission on Africa. The Commission's report integrates what Africa must do, what the rest of the world must do to support Africa and what the rest of the world must stop doing to remove the barriers to Africa's development. The vast majority of its more than eighty recommendations, which cover everything from mosquito nets to multilateral finance, are aimed at donor countries. Importantly, while it advocates a sharp escalation in aid to Africa, it admits that most African states do not have the capacity to absorb aid at present and the first tranches of aid must be used for capacity building. It admits that Western countries are involved in bribery and that much of the stolen and corrupt funds come to banks in British territories. They must be identified, frozen and returned. It accepts that churches in Africa have been the main deliverers of health and education.

The report recommends that aid to Africa be doubled in the short term and then tailed off in the second decade. It says aid should be better targeted and co-ordinated in support of Nepad and it should be a clear long-term commitment. It recommends 100 per cent debt relief for those countries that need it. While it recommends open markets for Africa's goods in the rest of the world, it says African countries do not have to reciprocate immediately if it will damage their own interests.

Will it work? The British hope that the Americans will still come on board despite their clear rejection of the International Finance Facility, the Commission's proposed vehicle for raising the extra aid now. But Washington accepts the need for debt relief. The Canadians, although more sympathetic, also reject the IFF. The French and Germans will back it and it is expected that the Italians will too. The Japanese will not wish to be left alone and out of step though they are not keen on debt relief. Critically, the window of opportunity is very narrow. Britain's chairmanship of the G8 in Gleneagles, Scotland, in July, will be followed in the years to come by Russia, Japan, Italy and Germany – none of whom have shown much interest in Africa.

But the report will give a hefty push to initiatives already in motion. Business in particular has taken up the cause and has become vigorously engaged with the deeper causes of Africa's poverty and the broader African agenda. There will be a better deal on debt. Although agricultural subsidies will not be removed in the short term, they have simply become politically and economically incorrect, indefensible except for the fact they are difficult to remove quickly. Above all, the report and the Commission have changed the image of Africa. It can no longer be referred to as a single, undifferentiated 'Hopeless Continent' (*The Economist*, cover story, 13 May 2000).

Africa, Dowden argued, will only work when Africans believe in Africa. When Africans invest in their own countries so will other investors. In the meantime, outsiders should follow the principle of doing no harm.

Sunday 1 May 2005

In the final session of the conference on 'Partnership and Trade', **Peter Draper** considered four thematic questions: What must Africa do to help itself? What can the developed world do? What can big developing countries do? What can South Africa do?

Draper argued that, generally, Africa's position in the global economy is tenuous. Even if developed country agricultural trade regimes were to be substantially dismantled in the Doha round, it is likely that most of the benefits would accrue to Cairns group agricultural exporters in Latin America, Australasia and South East Asia. On the other hand, current preferential access would be diminished, threatening vulnerable commodity exports, while potential price rises could contribute to food insecurity in several food importing states. Gains from industrial tariff liberalization would almost certainly accrue to efficient East Asian producers, especially China.

Faced with these prospects, African countries needed to focus on building their capacity to produce and trade goods. Crucially, this involves liberalizing imports of both goods and services to boost consumer demand, secure intermediate and capital goods inputs for production and underpin economic growth through provision of core infrastructure services. Good governance is a *sine qua non* for this to occur. Regarding development of supply-side capabilities, he highlighted three sets of interventions: building economic management institutions; developing both physical and financial infrastructure; and trade facilitation – especially regarding regional trade. Such an approach would support export diversification, but needed to be matched by commitments in both developed and big developing countries to reduce barriers to African exports, including reduction of trade distorting subsidies.

Draper argued that greater coherence between trade policy and poverty reduction strategy is essential, and that such initiatives must be locally owned and predicated on good governance. The current wave of regionalism could also undermine WTO disciplines and the multilateral trading system, with potentially dire consequences for African countries.

Noting that developing countries account for a substantial and increasing percentage of world trade, Draper pointed out that the big developing countries should do more to liberalize their trading regimes. But rather than base this on regional integration arrangements, thus contributing to the WTO's mounting problems, this should be based on unilateral trade liberalization. In the specific case of China, three issues required Beijing's attention: greater discipline on the operations of Chinese firms in Africa in order to ensure more ethical investment; alignment of China's aid programme in accord with the guidelines for aid dispersal and other programmes of the OECD Development Action Committee; and revaluation the Chinese currency to more realistic levels.

Finally, Draper outlined several ways in which South Africa could contribute to African development through trade, including unilateral trade liberalization and expansion of SACU, which would offer regional economic and diplomatic spin-offs as SA markets are not currently particularly open to its neighbouring states.

Ebrahim Ebrahim, meanwhile, argued that in both the security and economic contexts, external engagement with Africa must be done in a manner consistent with and supportive of the aims of Nepad.

Overall, the Dialogue reflected the growing international consensus around Africa's developmental challenges and the need to address them. Africa must take the lead in solving its own problems. The cornerstone of progress is good governance. It must also move beyond the propensity to see the forming of national, regional and continental institutions as solutions in and of themselves. While the growing integration of post-apartheid South Africa with the rest of the continent has seen a proliferation of new intra-continental economic and diplomatic structures, more emphasis must now be placed on making them function effectively. And, importantly, African governments need to recognize that regional institutions are not a substitute for strong states.

In its Fourth Round, the Tswalu Dialogue reinforced the constructive value of – and indeed the necessity for – forging consensus among diverse influential stakeholders in quiet, informal settings, where hard vested positions yield more easily to the recognition of shared interests and mutual respect.

Section 1

The Global Environment

Advancing Freedom, Peace and Prosperity in Africa: Statement by the United States Assistant Secretary of State for African Affairs

Jendayi Frazer

Her Excellency Dr Jendayi E. Frazer, (then) United States Ambassador to South Africa, delivered the opening address of the 2005 Tswalu Dialogue on 28 April 2005. At the time, there was intense speculation in Washington that President Bush would nominate Dr Frazer to be Assistant Secretary of State for African Affairs. Two months later she was formally nominated by the President for the position, and on the 22 July 2005 she appeared before the Senate Committee on Foreign Relations. In her Statement to the Committee, Dr Frazer addressed many of the same key issues she touched upon during her opening remarks at Tswalu. The US Senate unanimously confirmed her appointment as Assistant Secretary of State for African Affairs on 29 July 2005. What follows in an abridged version of her confirmation hearing statement.

The United States is fortunate in having broad bipartisan consensus on our Africa policy. I look forward to working with Congress and particularly the Senate Foreign Relations Committee to realize the opportunities this unique moment in history offers to advance freedom, peace, and prosperity in Africa.

I appeared before this committee exactly fifteen months ago as the President's nominee to become US Ambassador to South Africa. Over the past year, I have served with the dedicated women and men of the Foreign and Civil Services and the Foreign Service Nationals in our embassy in South Africa and at the State Department. I will be proud to lead the Department's Africa team of committed individuals both in the Bureau and especially those who serve in some of our most difficult and exciting posts overseas.

I have visited twenty-one of the forty-eight countries in sub-Saharan Africa, and worked on African issues for over twenty-five years moving between academia (as Assistant Professor at the University of Denver and at Harvard University), and government service (at the Joint Chiefs of Staff and National Security Council). I am especially proud to have served from 2001 to 2004 as Special Assistant to the President and Senior Director for African Affairs at the National Security Council where I had the opportunity to contribute to the United States Government's strong record of engaging Africa.

In all the years I have studied and worked on Africa I have not known a more auspicious time to consolidate the progress and promise of the continent. Democracy in Africa is growing with more than fifty democratic elections in the past four years. Economic growth on the continent is at an eight year high and twenty countries have registered growth for each of the past five years. Six major wars – Angola, Burundi, Democratic Republic of the Congo, Liberia, Sierra Leone, Sudan north-south – have progressed to post-conflict situations over the past five years. Africans are taking control of their destiny with the African Union and its New Partnership for Africa's Development (Nepad) programme of action contributing to better governance and friendlier ties among states.

Post 9/11, Americans also see more clearly the link between America's well-being and Africa's progress. Secretary of State Condoleezza Rice remarked recently in Senegal that opening our markets through AGOA benefits everyone. 'African businesses create more, better-paying jobs. And American consumers receive more goods at lower prices.' Africans are sharing the burden of maintaining international peace and security by supplying 30 per cent of United Nations peacekeeping forces worldwide with four African countries – Ethiopia, Ghana, Nigeria, and South Africa – among the top ten UN troop contributors. As we confront America's gravest threats of terrorism and proliferation of weapons of mass destruction, we find willing partners and ready models in Africa. In Africa, extreme poverty does not equate to extremist ideology. South Africa proves that abandoning nuclear weapons can enhance a country's global standing and influence. Africa's embrace of freedom and tradition of religious tolerance offers hope to the Greater Middle East.

I will increase American engagement in Africa guided by a clear understanding of these US interests. My vision and priorities for US Africa policy derive directly from President Bush's charge to make the world safer and better, and the Secretary's guidance that the State Department will pursue the goals in the National Security Strategy through transformational diplomacy. Translated to Africa, the key priorities are:

- First, to support the spread of political freedom throughout the continent;
- Second, to expand economic opportunity and growth;
- Third, to address the unique challenge of the HIV/AIDS pandemic; and
- Finally, to reinforce African initiatives to end conflict and fight terror.

Let me expand on each of these areas in turn:

Over the past fifteen years the trend line is excellent for the spread of freedom and democracy across the African continent. Elections have taken place widely. Power has changed hands in a number of key nations, from Senegal to Ghana, from Zambia to Madagascar. While there is no democracy deficit in Africa, there is still a ways to go as progress has been uneven, and at times, quite fragile. Transformational diplomacy requires moving beyond elections as the measure of freedom to support the efforts of African people to achieve real democracy through government accountability and effective and independent institutions. This demands:
- Speaking out loudly for liberty and against repression. In countries like Zimbabwe where there are grave human rights abuses, I will say so clearly and support the Zimbabwean people in their struggle for human dignity and to return democracy to their country.
- Continuing to build the institutions that are the essential components of a decent society: free press, an independent judiciary, a sound financial system, strong labour unions, and vibrant political parties.
- Strongly backing Nepad and its African Peer Review Mechanism to help African leaders to instil positive attitudes towards democracy and good governance among their peers.
- Providing, through the Millennium Challenge Account, the significant resources needed to encourage reform and assist those countries that are committed to good governance.

I aim to contribute to the great task set out by Secretary Rice for the State Department to 'unite the community of democracies in building an international system that is based on our shared values and the rule of law.'

Africa is a rich continent in an impoverished state. Therefore, my second priority is to expand economic opportunity, especially by unleashing the potential of Africa's own entrepreneurs. This objective is advanced by opening markets to create jobs; encouraging domestic reforms to support small- and medium-sized businesses; levelling the playing field in the global economic arena; and where necessary, providing development assistance as a catalyst for growth. The following two areas of action stand out:

- The African Growth and Opportunity Act (AGOA) will remain the centrepiece of the Administration's Africa economic policy to provide duty free access for most African countries to the $11 trillion US market.
- Encouraging domestic reform is also necessary to generate the jobs and resources essential for economic growth. African governments have to lessen regulatory and bureaucratic burdens on small and medium sized businesses. They also must act decisively to stamp out corruption that chokes the entrepreneurial spirit, and turns away potential investors.

President Bush has taken important steps over the past five years to level the playing field by pushing reform of the international financial institutions and World Trade Organization. American leadership was important for the G-8 to reach agreement on cancelling the debt of the Heavily Indebted Poor Countries (HIPC). I will continue to work closely with:

- Treasury Department to assist Africa in managing its debt and push the President's plan to end the destabilizing lend-and-forgive approach to development assistance in low-income countries.
- USTR to implement the WTO Doha Development Agenda and reduce trade barriers, especially eliminating agricultural export subsidies, reducing domestic supports, and improving market access.
- State and Treasury Departments to develop Africa's infrastructure in partnership with the private sector and collaboration with the Africa Development Bank and World Bank.

Finally, official development assistance (ODA) will continue to be needed in addition to pro-market policies, trade, and debt cancellation. ODA must become a catalyst for growth and development rather than a crutch engendering dependence. Since 2000, President Bush, with the support of the US Congress, has tripled ODA to sub-Saharan Africa and he promised to further double ODA to Africa. Much of the new assistance to Africa will be through the Millennium Challenge Account to ensure we work with reformers committed to increasing the opportunity for their peoples. Assistance will also go to support the empowerment of women and education of girls. I will work with African governments, local communities, and non-governmental organizations to promote sustainable development and build partnerships that protect Africa's environment, including providing assistance for better resource management, especially of water, forests, wildlife, fisheries and other resources, both bilaterally and in trans-boundary regions.

My most urgent priority will be to fight contagious diseases on the continent, especially the HIV/AIDS pandemic, tuberculosis and malaria. HIV/AIDS tears apart African families and destroys the hope of millions. This pandemic presents a unique challenge to Africa's future. Under the leadership of the President and with great support from Congress, the United States has taken the lead role in this global struggle. The President's Emergency Plan for HIV/AIDS Relief provides more resources than all other donors combined. The plan has transformed the world response and, most important, its success thus far has been based on the partnerships forged with African governments, private sector, faith-based and non-governmental organizations and academia. The next important step is to ensure that we institutionalize Africa's national health capacity. As Ambassador to South Africa, I have had an opportunity to directly lead the embassy team in this noble cause and I will bring a field perspective to my role as Assistant Secretary joining Ambassador Tobias and the Congress to prevent this disease from destabilizing African nations and undermining Africa's recent democratic and economic progress.

Finally, I will continue to back African conflict mediation and strengthen African capacity to carry out peace support operations. The Administration's approach to work with lead African mediators and multi-laterally with the United Nations, African Union, and sub-regional organizations like ECOWAS has worked. As Assistant Secretary I will ensure that the Africa Contingency Operations and Training Assistance (ACOTA) programme receives the necessary guidance, oversight and resources to contribute to Africa's stability. I will also work to strengthen the East Africa Counter-terrorism and the Trans-Sahara Counter-terrorism Initiatives to provide a robust and multifaceted programme to deny terrorists safe haven, operational bases, and recruitment opportunities in Africa. Outreach to Muslim communities and to African youth is critical to the success of our efforts. My focus will be working with the embassies and Ambassadors to not only shut down terrorist networks, but to offer a vision of hope and opportunity to eliminate the despair that can feed extremist ideologies. My most important responsibility is protecting

Americans abroad, and, working with Diplomatic Security and General Williams at Overseas Buildings Office (OBO), to ensure the safety and security of the approximately 12,700 USG officials and locally engaged staff serving at the forty-seven posts in sub-Saharan Africa.

In conclusion, it is not enough to list my priorities as Assistant Secretary. With limited resources and personnel and forty-eight countries to cover in sub-Saharan Africa, these four priorities must be strategically pursued. I aim to develop strategies to affect each of the four distinct sub-regions of Central, Western, Eastern and Southern Africa. In each sub-region I will focus engagement on the strong democratic reformers, countries like Senegal, Ghana, Mali and Benin, to illustrate in West Africa. It is also important to engage the continent's major powers, especially South Africa and Nigeria. They account for about 60 per cent of Sub-Saharan Africa's GDP, are the major contributors to African mediation and peacekeeping, and are the most influential countries in the African Union. I am confident in the success of our Africa policy and approach given the innovative initiatives and historic resources at hand. I am cognizant of the importance members of this Committee attach to US Africa policy. I look forward to working with you to realize our shared vision. Together we will advance freedom, peace and prosperity in Africa.

What the External Community can do for Africa: Assessing the Report of the Commission for Africa

Richard Dowden

Origins

Bob Geldof persuaded Tony Blair to set up the Commission for Africa. Blair had begun to show an interest in Africa towards the end of his first term as he sought a foreign policy issue for his second term. Africa had played very little part in the New Labour Project in its first term. It had been left to Clare Short at the Department for International Development, the old Overseas Development Administration, which was separated from the Foreign Office and given more money. British aid was untied and switched to budget support for governments. Aid was to be solely targeted on poverty reduction with the targets set by the Millennium Development Goals.

Despite a missionary spirit – Blair set out to 'save Africa', which he described as 'a scar on the conscience of the world' – he nonetheless showed little interest in engaging Africa experts. The process was driven by the aid industry – a combination of aid agencies, celebrities and the churches. They created the Jubilee Debt Campaign and Make Poverty History. This was not a constituency Blair wanted to alienate, but they focused primarily on raising money.

The Commission for Africa was the culmination of that process. It was an odd collection of seventeen people, the majority African but with three British ministers and a British secretariat. While the 1980 Brandt report, the conclusions of a Commission headed by the former West German Chancellor on the North-South divide, took retired statesmen seven years to deliberate the issues, the Commission was given in effect seven months to come up with answers.

Shortly after it began, Sir Nicholas Stern, a Treasury official, was drafted in to manage and write the report. Gordon Brown insisted that debt and aid were Treasury issues. For a moment it looked as if Geldof would walk out. But he stayed, and the Commission began a frantic round of consultations in Britain, Europe, Africa and elsewhere.

Achievements

I have been respectfully sceptical of the process. Respectful because it was not an easy task to push Africa to the top of the international agenda, and the effort stood a good chance of failing. But Blair did not give up or let it slide, and in Britain a huge new enthusiasm for Africa has been created. The BBC has devoted a whole season to Africa, the British Museum and art galleries all over the UK are full of Africa exhibitions and there are concerts, debates and discussions which have been very well attended.

But beneath the surface there were problems. The falling out of Blair and Mbeki over Zimbabwe deprived Blair of his most important ally in Africa. Many Africans were sceptical because of Blair's missionary language and more generally because of his support for the Iraq invasion. The choice of venue and timing of the launch on Red Nose Day, and the sudden change of date of the release of the report to suit Downing Street's news agenda all seemed to indicate that Africa still came second to the British government's own interests.

What it says

But perhaps these were minor irritants. The report itself is a remarkable document of 461 pages. Its greatest strength is that it is comprehensive. It integrates what Africa must do, what the rest of the world must do in support of Africa and what the rest of the world must stop doing to remove the barriers to Africa's development. The vast majority of its more than eighty recommendations, which cover everything from mosquito nets to multilateral finance, are aimed at donor countries.

It is honest about the causes of Africa's failure to develop. It admits that the world trade system is not the cause. It admits many African states do not have the capacity to absorb aid at present and the first tranches of aid must be used for capacity building. It admits that Western countries are involved in bribery and that much of the stolen and corrupt funds come to banks in British territories. They must be identified, frozen and returned. It accepts that churches in Africa have been the main deliverers of health and education.

It presents a coherent package of remedies. The report says: 'The problems they address are interlocking. They are vicious circles which reinforce one another. They must be tackled together. To do that Africa needs a comprehensive big push on many fronts at once.' There is no option to 'pick and mix' its recommendations.

It recommends that aid to Africa should be doubled in the first decade and then should tail off in the second. It says aid should be better targeted and co-ordinated in support of Nepad, and it should be a clear long-term commitment. It recommends 100 per cent debt relief for those countries that need it – a measure the G8 has since accepted, albeit with conditionalities. And recommends open markets for Africa's goods in the rest of the world, but says African countries do not have to reciprocate immediately if it will damage their own interests.

There is not much new in the report, as many have pointed out, but fortunately it did not try to invent a new magic bullet to solve Africa's problems.

At the launch, when Blair was asked if Britain accepted the report and would implement all the recommendations, he replied 'Yes'. The report is now official British policy.

Will it work?

This is the document that Blair is using to create the agenda at the G8 Summit in Gleneagles, Scotland in July, and will use when Britain takes the presidency of the EU in the second half of 2005.

The British seem to believe that the Americans will still come on board despite their clear rejection of the International Finance Facility, the Commission's proposed vehicle for raising the extra aid now. But the Americans accept the need for debt relief. The Canadians, although more sympathetic, also reject the IFF. The French and Germans will back it and, in theory, so do the Italians. The Japanese will not wish to be left alone and out of step though they are not keen on debt relief. It looks unlikely that any of these positions will change between now and 8 July. The G8 leaders will also want to use the report as a range of options – not a complete package as it is presented. So it is likely that although some recommendations may be acted upon, it will not amount to The Big Push that is called for.

The outlook for delayed implementation is not good. After Britain's chairmanship of the G8 comes Russia, then Japan, Italy and Germany – none of whom have shown much interest in Africa.

Assessment

But the report will give a hefty push to initiatives already in motion. Business in particular has taken up the cause and has become vigorously engaged with the deeper issues of Africa's poverty and the broader African agenda. In June a deal on debt was agreed at a G8 Finance Ministers meeting which agreed to write of the debts of eighteen Highly Indebted Poor Countries, fourteen of them in Africa, freeing up $1.5 billion for their governments. Although agricultural subsidies will not be removed in the short term, they have simply become politically and economically incorrect, indefensible except for the fact they are difficult to remove quickly. Above all, the report and the Commission have changed the image of Africa. It can no longer be referred to as a single, undifferentiated 'Hopeless Continent' as *The Economist* once described Africa.

The mistake at the heart of the report, in my view, and even more at the heart of the Sachs report – Investing in Development, the report on the Millenium Development Goals chaired by Jeffrey Sachs – is that they conflate the shrivelled African child dying in its mother's arms that we see on TV, with the wealthy African elites who own and run African countries. They are both referred to as the Africans. There is no analysis of the relationship between them.

The report's examples of Ghana, Mali and Ethiopia as evidence that the continent is reforming and aid is working are not sufficiently weighty in my view to justify a 'Big Push'. We all know excellent aid projects – usually small scale – so I am not saying that aid cannot work. It works well at the local level – as Africa does when it is allowed to. The conduct of the governments of Kenya, Côte d'Ivoire and Sudan, not to mention Zimbabwe, and the failure of the peace process to move further forward in the Democratic Republic of Congo, are to me strong counter-weights to the argument that things are getting better.

What can be done?

Africa will only work when Africans believe in Africa. This is where Fanon and finance meet. Perhaps the greatest damage colonialism and imperialism did to Africa was not political or economic. It destroyed Africa's self-belief. One indicator of that is the outflow of privately owned African capital. When Africans invest in their own countries so will others. At present only the biggest outside companies can afford to gamble in Africa. Things will only change, therefore, when Africa's elites are swept away in revolution, which seems unlikely, or when they come to see that the development of their own countries is in their own interest – when they commit to popular welfare.

In the meantime, outsiders should follow the principle of doing no harm. So I look forward to seeing Britain take a lead and signing up to the UN Convention on Corruption, pushing the 'Publish What You Pay' agenda, regulating arms dealers based in London and all the other small but important measures that hinder Africa's development. Last year Britain sold more than £1 billion ($1.7 billion) worth of arms to African governments.

It could also do much to revive tertiary education in Africa. Most important is to staunch the loss of Africa expertise inside and outside the continent. If we want to help Africa, the most important thing to do is to understand it.

Africa and the Global Environment: Is there a dramatic opportunity to change things?

John Battersby

In the debate which has gathered some momentum in recent months in Britain around the recommendations of the Africa Commission – the body appointed by British Prime Minister Tony Blair to boost the Nepad and the African Peer Review Mechanism (APRM) processes and devise concrete strategies for accelerating African development – the element of urgency is often stressed.

The argument goes that a unique confluence of initiatives and events has conspired to focus at last on the much neglected development of the African continent, and if Africa and its friends in the industrialized countries do not take full advantage of this opportunity now – during the course of this year – it might not come around again for another ten years, if ever.

Well, the cynics would say that is a bit melodramatic given all the false-starts on Africa and all the talk and so little action over the years. What has suddenly changed decades of indifference and handouts?

Africans, who are generally not cynical, might ask that, having waited all this time for a real engagement with the industrialized countries of the North, what has suddenly changed that has created this great sense of urgency? The reality is that the development of Africa is a process that will take decades and generations but desperately needs a global consensus and commitment that will enable the process to be kick-started and made sustainable.

African leaders such as President Thabo Mbeki and his fellow Nepad founders have argued that Nepad provides a framework for a partnership between African and industrialized countries – good governance in exchange for resources and engagement – but they would also say that Nepad is as much about changing attitudes and breaking with the patronizing hand-out mentality of the past as it is about addressing the north/south imbalance of resources.

It is in essence about having a meeting of minds which relegates to the past, the colonial era and its legacy.

But – to return to the issue of Africa's 'last chance' – it is true that in the complex world of global power shifts, there is an unusual constellation of events and initiatives which have provided a focus on African issues that have hitherto been marginalized by events in the Middle East – particularly Afghanistan and Iraq – in the post-9/11 era.

The reform of the United Nations institutions and the upcoming review of the Millennium Development Goals in September have set the backdrop for the year in which Britain chairs the G8 group for the first six months and the EU, whose Africa initiative stalled over Zimbabwe, for the second six months. Then there is the crucial meeting of the WTO in Hong Kong at the end of the year which provides a platform to complete the Doha round and accelerate the scrapping of agricultural and other subsidies.

All this provides Britain with an opportunity to lobby amongst its G8 partners and the EU for a greater focus on African development. Ironically, that greater focus was achieved at the G8 meeting in Kananaskis in Canada in 2002 but it has remained largely a paper agreement due to the international focus on the war in Iraq.

The Africa Commission, which has changed the language of African development, has provided useful mechanisms for speeding up development, costing the various initiatives proposed by Nepad, writing off debt, increasing aid and prioritizing higher education and the strengthening of African universities has successfully provided the context for this confluence of activities.

Ahead of the G8 meeting in Gleneagles there will need to be some intense partnership building to reconnect the Africa Commission process, which some newcomers have tended to see as the Holy Grail, and the Nepad process which was adopted after two years of lobbying by African leaders and given some more substance at Evian, France in 2003.

African leaders are determined to retain control of the new partnership because its strength is that it is a home-grown African initiative and will need to remain so if it is going to be effective in the long run. That will mean channelling funds through African institutions such as the African Development Bank and using institutions such as the UN Economic Commission for Africa to guide the process.

But there are other important global factors which have conspired to create an opportunity to focus the international community's attention and resources on the issue of African development. These include:

- The 9/11 attack on the United States and the ensuing debate which has brought home in the minds of many thought leaders the inextricable link between fundamentalism and terrorism, on the one hand, and poverty, underdevelopment and failed states on the other hand.
- The global response to the 2004 tsunami in Asia and its contribution to the realization of one inter-connected humanity – that ultimately we are all dependent on each other in an increasingly globalized world and that global security is increasingly based on eliminating the massive imbalances that will create flows of poor jobless people to the industrialized world, and that an unchecked global AIDS pandemic could result in a string of dependent failed states in Africa and even in Asia.
- The rise of China as a global economic power and its rapidly developing trade and investment relationship with Africa, which is an increasingly important source of the oil, steel and strategic minerals that China needs to feed its voracious economy.

It is this last issue – the rise of China in Africa – that I would like to focus on for the rest of this paper.

One of the last trips I participated in as political editor of the Independent Group of newspapers in South Africa in late 2003 was a ten-day visit to China at the invitation of the Chinese Government as part of a delegation of eighteen African journalists from eleven African countries. It was a most instructive trip, and it changed my view both of the world and of Africa's role and relationship with the international community.

Mixing with a diversity of African colleagues from countries such as the Seychelles, Ethiopia, Ghana, Kenya and Zimbabwe, I realized that culture and national interests in Africa are as divergent as people from different parts of Europe or different parts of Asia. But I also became more aware of the traits, cultural commonalities and qualities that belong to Africa in a broader sense and bind Africans into a people distinct from Europeans, Americans or Asians.

On the other hand, we will all be familiar with those qualities which could be said to make up the African brand. Emphasis on family ties and communal support, the culture of innovation and improvisation, the centrality of art, dance and music, and the culture of agency – the extraordinary inclination of Africans abroad to repatriate a portion of their earnings, resources and human capital to support their family, clan, community and nation.

In what has become known in the Cold War era as 'the West' (in relation to eastern Europe or the communist block) – but can probably now be more accurately described as the industrialized north – we will also be familiar with the stereotypes which have sought to characterize the more negative brand image of Africa: conflict, poverty, underdevelopment, famine, disease, failed states and military dictatorships.

But the most interesting insight of the trip was to see how China views and deals with Africa and how Africans perceive and deal with China. China perceives Africa as a continent of untapped potential offering a future partnership of great promise. Africans tend to see China more as a developed, rather than a developing, country because of the sheer scale of its economic growth, but they are more than happy to do business with such a willing and powerful partner, whatever the cultural gulf might be.

So when one is talking about the global environment, the rise of China as a major global economic power and, in particular, the growing trade and investment relationship between China and Africa is the central issue. It is true that China, which traditionally takes a long-term and strategic view while at the same time retaining the capacity for radical and intensely pragmatic short-term adjustments, has been developing its relationships with post-colonial African states since the early 1960s.

But in the past decade, which like the one before it has been characterized by rates of growth averaging 10 per cent, the strategic relationship between China and Africa has taken on a far greater significance. In one sense, China's objectives in Africa are no different from those of other powers: We will provide the manufactured goods in return for access to resources – oil, steel and other strategic minerals – for which the Chinese economic machine has developed an apparently insatiable appetite.

But China's need is arguably both greater and more immediate than the other major powers: in order to feed its 1.2 billion people, it needs to maintain a double-digit growth rate. Chinese leaders have worked on a three-year food supply to keep the dragon from the door. It is a matter of collective survival which – as those who have visited China will know – takes clear precedence over the survival of the individual. The strategic and philosophical approach adopted by China is fundamentally different from the Western industrialized countries, which have linked their aid and investment policies in Africa to good governance, democratic accountability and economic liberalization.

China takes a more pragmatic – and some would say opportunistic or even amoral – view. But it also sets greater store in building enduring long-term relationships than in transaction-based business, which is the norm in the West. Rover has discovered this recently at some considerable cost.

China engages with countries regardless of governance and human rights issues – good examples here are China's involvement in developing the oil industry in Sudan despite charges of genocide being levelled against the government in Khartoum for the alleged ethnic cleansing of African Muslims in Darfur. Another example would be Zimbabwe, where China's public engagement has been unaffected by EU and US sanctions against the Mugabe government. That does not mean that China does not care about human rights violations. It takes a different philosophical approach of long-term relationship building and then using that relationship both to secure its long-term economic interests as well as influencing political issues.

Regardless of whether such an approach is right or wrong in terms of the value systems of Western democracies, there is a new reality which the West/North is going to have to face: the pace at which China is investing in and trading with Africa is fast undermining the traditional influence of the former colonial powers in Africa – France and Britain – and changing the relationship between the world's major military superpower, the United States, and the rapidly emerging superpower on the other side of the Pacific – the People's Republic of China. The battleground, unsurprisingly, will be around control of the supply, and therefore, the price of crucial resources and, in particular, energy – oil and nuclear power.

It is no secret that the continued dominance of the US as a global power – underpinned by its military-industrial establishment – is based on access to cheap energy and preventing other states from acquiring nuclear power for military use. In respect of oil, Africa has become a key resource in case of disruption in the flow of Middle Eastern oil. It provides the best option of a reliable alternative supply of oil. So, when China invests in oil in the Sudan, it has notched one up over the US.

In that respect, although much has been made of the confrontation between Islam and the West and the war against terrorism, it is essentially a side-show in the looming battle for global power and resources between the US military-industrial establishment and a rapidly growing China. Where does this leave Africa in relation to the global environment? Well, I would suggest that it changes the picture fundamentally. It offers Africa another route to rapid development.

When China decides to invest substantial sums in a plant for the mass manufacture of motorbikes in Angola, it is way ahead of Britain,

France and the US in its long-term thinking. The economy of Vietnam, once a country of bicycles and agricultural self-sufficiency, is now the world's second largest exporter of rice and its streets are flowing rivers of motorbikes, a key instrument of the country's industrialization.

When the CEO of one of Britain's largest banks announces incredulously that the majority of the bank's branches in Africa now have a separate China desk to deal with its growing transactions on the continent, then you know there is a fundamental change taking place in the global economy and Africa's place in it. All this gives a very different meaning to Afro-Asian solidarity. Fifty years ago in Bandung, Indonesia, when the Non-Aligned Movement (NAM) was created, it was about the oppressed peoples of the third world standing together in the face of the seemingly invincible economic and political domination of the colonial powers.

Today, as African and Asian leaders marked the event, the leading Asian powers – India and China – are emerging as global powers in their own right and offer a model of development which offers Africa far greater prospects of success than playing by the rules of the former colonial powers and the US, which refuses to bow on issues such as global warming and nuclear power and is slow to concede on trade subsidies.

As President Mbeki noted in his keynote speech during an official visit to Singapore recently:

> The process of democratization [in Africa] is irreversible. Africans are now building a peaceful and stable continent by dealing swiftly with incidents of conflict and instability as well as creating strong institutions for this purpose.

In a speech entitled *Africa's New Season of Hope: Dawn of a New Africa-Asia Partnership*, Mbeki stressed that for Africa's plan to succeed it needed to build strong partnerships – not only with the developed countries – but also with other African countries, other developed countries and between Africa and Asia. It is in this spirit that the important trilateral commission between South Africa, India and Brazil was formed nearly two years ago – a development which has attracted minimal attention in the developed world.

However, if these new rules pan out, Africa is going to be an increasingly important player because of its natural resources and strategic minerals, and because it offers the last untapped markets for global consumer growth. Between then and now lies a massive gulf between perceptions and reality in Africa. When the reality is that companies operating in Africa enjoy among the highest returns on their investment – just ask the CEO of Celtel for starters – why is the perception the opposite?

In his speech in Singapore, President Mbeki quoted the memoirs of Lee Kuan Yew in which he spoke of 'the long, hard slog ... against insuperable odds to make it from poverty to prosperity ... and build a multiracial society that would give equally to all its citizens regardless of race, language or religion'.

Under the leadership of Mbeki, Africa has embarked on that road.

African Stand-by Forces

Andrew Stewart

The African Union (AU) is a regional organization in terms of Article VIII of the UN Charter and has defined for itself the role of assuming 'overall responsibility for promoting peace, security and stability in Africa'.[1] Furthermore, one of the New Partnership for Africa's Development's (Nepad) priorities is to 'establish the conditions for sustainable development by ensuring peace and security'. More recently, Africans have clearly stated their desire to build sufficient capacity to be able to resolve conflicts in Africa themselves. The result has been a very ambitious agenda for the AU, defined in 2002, to establish an African Peace and Security Architecture (APSA) based on five sub-regional organizations. Each of those organizations is required to provide a brigade at thirty days, in some circumstances even at fourteen days, notice to move for the African Stand-By Force (ASF) by 2010.

Conceptually, APSA and the establishment of ASF take account of the comprehensive nature of effective conflict prevention, management and resolution. Provision is made for the development of African conflict prevention/mediation tools, civilian and military instruments of crisis management and post-conflict requirements. However, reality is a long way short of the concept. Rather, the uneven state of governance within Africa, the limited capacity of national armed forces and slow regional integration – to say nothing of the AU's current lack of political/military planning capability – points to the need for substantial external assistance, both financial and conceptual.

Amongst the most crucial requirements before AU aspirations can be reached are: regular and standardized training based on harmonized doctrine; strategic lift; sustainable logistic support; and clear command arrangements under political control from the AU through Regional

---

[1] cf. 2002 Durban Protocol.

Commands. One only has to recall how NATO during the Cold War (an alliance of fourteen developed and rich nation states facing an existential threat of national survival) had difficulty in reaching consensus, to see that the AU (a loose confederation of fifty-three under-developed and poor states facing predominantly intra- rather than inter-state conflicts) faces really significant problems in meeting its ASF goal. Pragmatism must win over ambition. A longer view must be taken. In all likelihood the AU mission to Darfur and its evolution over the next few months will demonstrate this. It will also highlight the reluctance of the developed world to provide peacekeepers in Africa.

Since the 2002 decisions there has been varied progress across Africa, but much is already being done, both bilaterally and at a regional level:

- The US is actively building African capacity for peace support training and associated logistics through its African Contingency Operations Training and Assistance (ACOTA) training programme. While the US European Command (EUCOM) leads, it and other departments from both DoD and State have over $600 million to spend in Africa this year.
- France is helping build capacity primarily through its Reinforcement of African Peacekeeping Capacities (RECAMP) exercises, but has over 300 personnel on the continent both to support this effort and to provide assistance bilaterally. She is also building a new tactical level Peace Support Training Centre in Bamako.
- The UK has a number of permanently deployed training teams in Sub-Saharan Africa, in addition to assistance provided to the AU, the Economic Community of West African States (ECOWAS) and the Intergovernmental Authority on Development with its Eastern African Standby Brigade (IGAD/EASBRIG). This assistance is mainly channelled through the Africa Conflict Prevention Pool (ACPP) that brings together three UK government departments (Department for International Development, Foreign and Commonwealth Office and Ministry of Defence) and which is worth £60 million per annum. Common funding leads to common policy between the departments.
- The US, France and the UK speak regularly to each other to try to de-conflict and co-ordinate. This difficult co-ordination function is increasingly shifting to Africa, where the AU will be hosting biannual donor conferences. The regional commands are also beginning to establish dialogue with key donor partners.

- Other countries are actively engaged in peace support capacity-building and governance, for example: Belgium, Canada, Norway and the Netherlands.
- The EU has come up with a number of initiatives to support the AU in the field of peace and security, including through the European Peace Facility (worth €250 million) and the use of its ESDP instruments, for example in the context of Darfur and the Democratic Republic of Congo.

Further evidence of progress is seen through projects that benefit from external support. These include:
- The Kofi Annan Peacekeeping Training Centre (KAIPTC) in Accra, which is co-financed together with the Ghanaian government by Canada, Germany, France, Italy, Japan, the Netherlands and UK. The KAIPTC acts as an ECOWAS Centre of Excellence, offering mission-oriented operational level PSO training to African forces. It also conducts research into the various aspects of PSO.
- The Tactical Peacekeeping Training School in Koulikouro (soon to move to its new premises in Bamako) which is co-financed together with the Malian government by France, the Netherlands, Switzerland and the UK. It offers bilingual (French and English) tactical training for African forces in PSO.
- The International Mine Action Training Centre (IMATC) in Nairobi, which is co-financed together with the Kenyan government by the UK. The IMATC was opened in February 2005. It can accommodate more than 200 students and trains African de-miners from all over the continent prior to PSO deployments.
- The building of the planning element premises for EASBRIG in Nairobi, Kenya by the UK government.

As political reality has started to bite (Darfur, Côte d'Ivoire, Liberia, Togo, Burundi, Somalia), the AU and sub-regional organizations have recognized the need for more rapid action. This is evident with their March 2005 'Roadmap on the Operationalization of the ASF', shared with the G8 and other partner countries at a joint meeting on 4 April 2005 in Addis Ababa. The AU has clearly identified the need to work with partners if the ASF is to move forward. To that end, a number of workshops are to be established, covering the essential issues of doctrine, SOPs, C3IS, logistics, training and evaluation.

It will now be necessary to take this positive momentum further. With Prime Minister Tony Blair making Africa a focus of the UK's G8 and EU Presidencies in 2005, little time can be wasted if advantage is to be taken of this focus. Following recent consultations with the AU and sub-regional organizations, the G8 are likely to adopt at the Gleneagles Summit in July a package of additional commitments, including in the fields of logistic support for the ASF, civilian police training, conflict prevention and post-conflict reconstruction. The G8 will also fully support the series of workshops that are being planned in the framework of the 'Roadmap' by the AU and regional organizations before the end of the year.

Improved co-ordination must form a key part of the Gleneagles package since it is evident that resources are limited and partner support will only be truly effective if co-ordinated properly. This applies not only to building peace-support capacity, but also the essential linkage between security, governance and economic development. If partner assistance is to be enduring, all future action needs to show African ownership. Indeed, it is the firm belief of the G8, that the AU and sub-regional organizations must take a lead in this process. The evolution of the APSA and ASF was in response to this demand. To that end, we need to welcome the fact that African leaders are increasingly demonstrating not only the determination but also some success in mediating with conflicting parties, as shown in recent crises.

On the surface, signs for the future look good. Africans want and indeed feel obliged to take ownership of their future and the G8 Summit will almost certainly demonstrate that partners stand ready to help. The real issue is whether both sides – the Africans and their partners – have the realism, patience, political will and staying power to meet the vision currently proposed. Without those determining factors there is a danger that in Africa there will continue to be much activity but little progress. All parties need to recognize that 'Ends, Ways and Means' need to be in balance.

Taking the ASF as an example, achieving the 'End' of five regional, high readiness, fully trained, sustainable brigades subject to political direction from the AU will take longer than four years. This is because the 'End' depends on the 'Means': here, principally resources, training and the necessary political/military security structures. Ideally, each region would have all its own equipment, strategic lift and logistic support established in a local depot. However, this would be hugely expensive for the partners unless they provided second-hand equipment coming to the end of its useful life. But that is not what the Africans want. They know from current experience that they cannot meet the maintenance and training bill. Furthermore, how likely is it that five concurrent, brigade-sized operations could be controlled, even if there was the demand? Is national role specialization an option or would that leave ASF brigades hostage to fortune? What if the nation in which the depot sat was not prepared to support the intended deployment? Political and military realities, therefore, indicate that there are few 'Means' currently available. The 'Means' determine the 'Ways' of reaching to the 'End'. Until those 'Means' are available the pragmatic solution may be to adjust the 'End'.

Truly building African capacity to that envisaged by the AU is probably a thirty-year project. We must therefore be realistic and concentrate on where we can make a difference. To use a military principle, we should reinforce success, not failure. This suggests the need for a building-block approach. For the development of the ASF, one would first look at national capacity. Each nation should be able to deploy its troops trained to a common standard, medically fit and with personal equipment. The best way of doing this is on a bilateral basis as exemplified by the France/Senegal, UK/Ghana or Belgium/Benin relationships. Perhaps each African nation could have a 'lead' partner responsible for this first building block.

The next building block is that of the development of the regional organizations. This is not a bilateral issue for partners, but one where they should closely co-ordinate their efforts. It is already happening in ECOWAS where France, the UK and the US have all attached officers to the HQ in Abuja. However, it needs to happen across the whole of Africa wherever that is politically possible. In some circumstances there will be constraints; the Southern African Development Community – on paper the most capable and richest regional organization – is being hampered by partners' restricted ability to assist in light of the political situation in Zimbabwe. However, that is reality and there is a need to accept that each regional organization will move at a different pace. The Africans must also see that success breeds greater investment.

The third level is the AU, which still needs to tackle a number of political and legal questions related to the command and control of the ASF. Only the Africans can lead on this, but they do need to understand the art of the possible. That will demand real co-ordination between the AU and the G8 and other partners. It will also need some straight talking on both sides and some hard listening. The meetings in Addis Ababa over the last two months indicate that the AU is recognizing its responsibilities. It is now up to the G8 to confirm how it can help. This will need collaboration rather than competition between nations. The Gleneagles Summit will be proof of how committed partners are to making AU ambitions a reality.

Africa's Challenges as Global Challenges, and the Viability of Nepad to Address Them

Shannon Field

The current global threats and challenges that we face as the international community have never before been so interdependent. As the UN High Level Panel on the subject recently noted, the mutual vulnerability of the weak and the strong has never been clearer. No state can alone make itself invulnerable to threats – a threat to one is a threat to all. The security of the most affluent state being held hostage to the ability of the poorest state to contain an emerging disease is a case in point. Among the most pressing threats that we currently face are: poverty, disease, environmental degradation, conflict, and terrorism.

The indispensable foundation for a collective security system to confront these threats is *development*. Development helps to combat poverty, reduce disease, protect the environment, address the root causes of civil war, and reduces the factors that give rise to terrorism. Poverty does not cause terrorism, but it is a base that cultivates its causes. We must therefore address, as a matter of urgency, the conditions which give rise to global imbalance and which breed a sense of anger, hopelessness, and frustration. The underprivileged do not necessarily form or lead terrorist movements, but those movements draw their foot soldiers from poorer regions where people feel marginalized. A more equitable distribution of resources and progress on meeting the Millennium Development Goals can contribute to making the world a safer place.

Africa suffers more than any other region of the world from the most prominent threats mentioned. Africa is the continent hardest hit by poverty, and all indications are that poverty is increasing. The number of people living on less than US$1 a day has increased since 1990, with currently 40 per cent of Africans living at this level. Some 140 million Africans are illiterate and the average life expectancy has declined from 50 to 46 since 1990. One in ten children die before the age of five, undernourishment has increased, and the number of deaths from HIV/AIDS has outstripped the number of deaths in all the civil wars fought in the 1990s.

HIV/AIDS is a transnational security threat which is being exacerbated by a worsening public health crisis. This is having a severe impact on Africa's labour markets, agricultural production and social services. The absence of health facilities in many African countries has led to a proliferation of malaria, and partial treatment has enabled new strains of tuberculosis to emerge that are harder to treat. What is urgently needed is to build local and national public health systems to confront these challenges. To add to these concerns, Africa's share of world trade has also declined to less than 2 per cent.

Nepad, as the socio-economic development programme for the African continent, is thus central to the objective of neutralizing these continental threats, which ultimately threaten global peace and security. It is important to recognize that Nepad is not an implementing agency. Nepad is a catalyzing, co-ordinating, mobilizing, unblocking and energizing agent. It is a vision for the continent, a framework and a programme within which others act, such as member states, the regional economic communities, the continental institutions and regional partners.

Nepad has built on a number of other initiatives devised to address the issue of under-development, such as the Financing for Development meeting in Monterrey, Mexico, which produced an ambitious programme to alleviate poverty, improve food security and protect the environment. Nepad also informed the UN Millennium Declaration which set targets and benchmarks that were consolidated in the Millennium Development Goals (MDGs). These include halving extreme poverty by 2014, protecting the environment and reversing the spread of HIV/AIDS.

Key to the realization of the MDGs will be for African governments to place them at the centre of their national poverty reduction strategies. African countries need to integrate their national and sub-regional plans within the framework of Nepad, and to align their budgets with Nepad priorities to meet the MDGs. A major challenge will be to mobilize the requisite resources to fund the Nepad programmes and projects.

To make Nepad viable, responsibility lies both with African governments and the international donor community. African governments need to develop an environment conducive for private sector growth, ensure responsible institutions, and invest in social services. Developed nations also need to do their part by reducing tariff barriers, increasing overseas development assistance (ODA), and providing debt relief and cancellation. A number of positive achievements relating to Nepad have already taken place, which include:

- The setting up of the implementation framework (including the AU organs and Nepad structures).
- The operationalization of the African Peer Review Mechanism (APRM).
- The resolution in various instances of conflict and instability in Africa.
- The development of key sectoral action plans and strategies.
- The identification of priority programmes and projects in various fields.
- The mobilization of human, institutional and financial resources in support of implementation.
- The mobilization of the international community in support of Nepad's implementation.

It is encouraging that despite the war in Iraq and international attention on terrorism, development assistance to Africa has increased from US$17.73 billion in 2001 to US$24 billion in 2003. More attention is now being paid to Africa's identified priorities such as agriculture and infrastructure. While progress is being made, there is a need for the G8 and the EU to align their assistance to Nepad. An important milestone in this regard has been the conclusions of the British Commission for Africa (CFA) Report released on 11 March 2005, which reiterates the key messages Nepad has been advocating over the past three years.

The Nepad Steering Committee has welcomed the Report's calls for the enhancement of resource inflows, debt cancellation, fostering the realization of Doha and greater market access for African countries. The report adds concrete detailed actions to the direction recommended by the Report of the UN Millennium Project, and offers proposals on how Africa can get back on track to achieving the MDGs. Specified funding requirements accompany these proposals. Many of the recommendations of the Report are synonymous with what has been proposed by Nepad.

A concern of the CFA is that at the current rates of progress, some of the MDGs will not be met until 2150. The annual amount that the CFA estimates the continent will need to effectively combat HIV/AIDs is US$10 billion, and a doubling of spending on infrastructure is deemed essential. The CFA has thus called for an additional US$25 billion in 2010, which represents a doubling of current aid levels, and a further US$25 billion by 2015. Rich nations are called on to commit to a timetable for giving 0.7 per cent of their annual income in aid. Aid must be long term, predictable and untied according to the Report. It recommends that aid should increasingly be given in the form of grants, and should be aligned with government priorities.

The Commission makes a useful suggestion that additional finances could be raised through an International Financing Facility, and international levies, such as a tax on airline tickets that could provide revenue for development. The proposal for an International Financing Facility has been welcomed by the Nepad Steering Committee as the most advanced and technically feasible proposal in terms of revenue generation. The major challenge in terms of realizing such a proposal will be to convince major powers such as the US of its necessity. To date, the US has ruled out contributing to such an initiative, with President George W Bush claiming that the US cannot commit due to the fact that, 'our laws are such that the legislature cannot commit the nation's funds many years into the future'.

The Report also calls on the West to abolish trade distorting subsidies to agriculture, lower tariffs and non-tariff barriers, and insists that the West must not demand reciprocal concessions from African countries. With the removal of trade barriers the Report argues that there needs to be a successful completion of the Doha Round, with time-bound goals for ending developed country protectionism and subsidies. These are issues that African countries have been raising consistently for years.

The Report acknowledges that not all African states have the governance, administrative and technical capacity to absorb substantive new inflows of aid. What is proposed to address this challenge is an approach whereby for the first three to five years, one third of new revenue for development would come from African sources through higher revenues, growth and better administration. The remaining two thirds would be financed by the international community through increases in aid. In the first stage there would be an assessment of governance and absorptive capacity, as well as revenue generation. At the end of three years a major review of progress and governance would take place to determine if further expansion of aid can be digested. These are important suggestions as African states do need a dramatic expansion of human capacity in order to effectively deliver services. In many countries there is a shortage of managers in most line ministries.

The debt burden is also a major emphasis of the report, noting that in recent years for every US$1 given in aid, nearly 50c has gone to rich nations in debt-service payments. The majority of this debt is public sector debt. The Report therefore recommends that developed nations should cancel debt stock and service up to 100 per cent, and cover multilateral and bilateral debt.

While the Report has come at a critical time, and has the potential to rally the international donor community behind Nepad's priorities, its utility can only be measured by the extent to which its recommendations are translated into delivery. British Prime Minister Tony Blair will have to sell his proposals to the G8 meeting this year. Without buy-in from this constituency of the world's largest and most developed economies, it will be hard to see how the MDGs can be achieved in Africa by the target dates set.

It will also be important for Britain and the other G8 nations to take the necessary policy decisions in their own countries so that African growth and development are not negated. Britain is one of the main Western recruiters of African trained health workers. This will need to be reversed if African investments in the health sector are to be worthwhile, and the goal of training an additional million health workers by 2015 is to be for the benefit of Africa's health systems. Trade negotiations with African countries will also need to prioritize African development as opposed to European advantage. Pressuring African governments to open up their markets to free trade deals could be devastating for agricultural industries. Similarly, if conflict prevention programmes within Nepad are to be effective, European countries will need to stem the flow of arms to state and non-state actors. According to Action Aid, in 2003, fourteen African countries were affected by wars, and ten of those countries had bought arms from Britain.

Most importantly, rich countries need to set a timetable for achieving their long-standing and long-unfulfilled commitment to devote 0.7 per cent of GNP as official development assistance by 2015. Germany recently announced a timetable to reach the target, and joins six other countries with such timetables: Belgium, Ireland, France, Spain and the UK. Countries like Canada, however, currently give approximately 0.3 per cent. This type of shortfall is unfortunate as Canada's 2005 shortfall (approximately $5 billion this year) would be enough to fund an entire global initiative to control malaria in Africa, a disease that kills more than 2 million children a year.

The question is not, therefore, whether Nepad as a socio-economic development programme is viable, but whether there is sufficient international political will to make the resources available. African nations have indicated their willingness to devote greater domestic resources to development. In response to the call by Nepad, African governments recently made a commitment to increase investment in agriculture to 10 per cent of national budgets over five years and monitor progress on an annual basis. The underlying principle of Nepad is the forging of a partnership between Africa and the developed countries. The extent to which this partnership is operationalized will determine how effectively the international community addresses the root causes of the challenges that threaten our collective security and prosperity. Humanity is, after all, indivisible.

The Changing Security Environment
Christopher Coker

One of the best ways to appreciate the future is to read novels, for novelists sometimes have a more penetrating insight into our world than do most political scientists.

One such novel is *Virtual Light* by William Gibson, the man who is credited with inventing the term 'cyberspace' in 1973. Since then he has become one of our leading science fiction writers. In *Virtual Light* Gibson takes us into a networked world in which the state has surrendered power to global corporations. At their head is Dat-America, which operates a surveillance system above the Earth that tracks the world's terrorists day and night. His dystopian vision of the future offers us the underside of globalization as we are beginning to experience it today: a world in which the social reality of the rich is utterly different from that of the poor. The rich live in video-monitored fortresses. Outside the public space is occupied by the poor, and defended by force of arms. The world is divided between what Manuel Castells calls 'the information rich' and 'the information poor'. The poor quite literally have been 'switched off'. They are useless on a labour market geared increasingly towards the production, processing and consumption of information.

Gibson is extrapolating from the present. This is what all science fiction writers do; they take present trends and project them into the future. His universal surveillance system is based on the Global Information Infrastructure Project launched by Al Gore when he was Vice President. The new challenges (the 'universe of potentials out there' – to quote Tom Ridge) are ones we monitor every day. Surveillance is a trademark of the risk societies we have become.

And there are other features of Gibson's world which might strike a chord with his readers. The top 1 per cent of the world's population now earns as much as the bottom 57 per cent and it is not surprising that the public spaces – or pre-modern enclaves in the first world, or pre-modern societies outside it, breed violence on a large scale.

Gibson's world is also one in which growing inequality leads to many conflicting orders – a world of undifferentiated jurisdictions between global corporations, drug cartels, militant nationalists and above all, terrorists.

The global surveillance network of Gibson's imagination is already here, in its incipient, domestic form. We should know it, most immediately, from what is happening to policing in the West. For we have gone from community policing to policing 'communities of risk' – those groups that are deemed to constitute a potential hazard. 'Zero tolerance' means moving potential criminals out of zones of most concern, such as areas of wealth creation and tourism. The CCTV camera has become the symbol of self-help. My own country, the UK, has more cameras per head of population than any other in the world. Most Britons are on camera most of their lives.

When criminals are apprehended they are imprisoned, usually for a long time. Our prison populations are larger than ever before: one prisoner for every 120 citizens in the United States. And the sentences are savage: 'three strikes and you're out' is now the norm. The old nineteenth century idea of rehabilitating the criminal, let alone redeeming him, has given way to locking him away, or quarantining him from the rest of us. Even when let out, they are electronically tagged so that their movements can be monitored.

If surveillance has become the vehicle of risk management at home, it is also becoming the vehicle of global management abroad. When rogue states are identified they are designated members of 'risk groups', and are subject to surveillance by satellite. Variously described as 'rogues', 'pariahs', 'outlaws' or more euphemistically 'states of concern', they are subject to round the clock satellite monitoring. And of course, they are assessed by experts as to the urgency of the threat they pose. Hence the debate on Iraq's Weapons of Mass Destruction.

Security

None of us seem to be very secure either in our immediate circumstances or our belief in the future. The extent of our present anxiety is caught by another novelist, James Blinn. 'What am I afraid of?' asks a character in one of his books, a pilot on an American aircraft carrier heading towards the Gulf in the First Gulf War, in this the first conflict to be televised in real time:

> I'm afraid of everything. You think war scares me? It does but so does nuclear winter and fallout from Chernobyl and legionnaires disease and killer bees... and crude nuclear devices, and strip-mining, and the vanishing rainforest, and AIDS... and rising interest rates and falling interest rates and people with accents and Third World population growth... and botulism and E-coli and unnamed Amazonian viruses, and the little petro-skin floating on my coffee.

The hero of Blinn's novel is a vivid example of a man who does not feel secure in himself, and certainly not the world around him. He is frightened by everything, what we call 'hard' and 'soft' security issues alike. He does not distinguish between them, even if we do. And he may well be right. For whether something is 'soft' or 'hard' is largely a matter of perception, not objective reality, and security today is based increasingly on subjective beliefs.

He is insecure, in part, because he no longer trusts the nation-state to secure him, his interests or even his beliefs. Once the most formidable political unit devised, now we have to draw a distinction between national security and homeland security, between the security of the state, and the security of the citizen, between aggression from another state and aggression from other citizens in far distant parts of the globe. National security still relies on military defence, including SDI shields. But how do you secure your citizen against everyday risks which involve other 'wars' – the 'war against terror', the 'war against crime', the 'war against AIDS'? How can a space-based anti-ballistic missile shield protect the citizen from crime when criminal gangs can operate almost without impediment across 6,000 miles of frontier, and 300 points of entry through which 500 million people passed in 2001?

If Blinn's hero feels at risk from so many forces he cannot understand – forces he cannot always put a name to – this is hardly surprising. He does not, for a start, buy into the language of 'soft' and 'hard' security, and may be quite wise not to: why should terrorism be a 'hard' issue, and crime a 'soft'? Transnational organized crime now accounts for about 8 per cent of world GNP. Setting aside the cost to governments, we also know that that it accounted for about 20,000 deaths a year in the Schengen-NAFTA area last year, a far higher figure than the number of casualties lost to terrorist acts. Yet, although we talk of a 'war on crime', states do not attach the same importance they do to the 'war against terrorism'. Most prefer to see crime as a law enforcement issue. But can the two be distinguished?

Was the Beslan school tragedy, for example, paid for by Bin Laden?

It is a question that was asked at the time. And it is not surprising it was asked, considering the fact that in 1998 he outbid a British company that offered $4 million for the safe return of four of its employees. Even if Bin Laden was not involved, it is impossible to divorce the Beslan incident from the buoyant war economy that has grown up in the Caucasus, now a hub in the region for counterfeiting dollars, money-laundering and kidnapping, all of which finance insurgent movements. Or put another way, crime both creates the demand for terrorism and supplies it at the same time.

No wonder in this kaleidoscopic security environment private security has become a growth industry. Ten years ago, only four US universities offered courses devoted to disaster management. Today, 115 degree courses are available and a further 100 are under consideration. On the internet you can find 24 hour status alerts against terrorism, and emergency supplies of potassium iodine for those who fear running short during a nuclear attack. The idea of self-help reminds me of the adverts in the early 1960s for 'deluxe fallout shelters' for middle-class families, offering every consumer comfort including wall-to-wall carpeting, lounge chairs and latest state-of-the-art TV. Sold to the public as a family room during peacetime and a fallout shelter should war break out, it offered the consumer protection against nuclear war providing you could pay the price. Here, wrote Herbert Marcuse in his book *One Dimensional Man*, was the introduction of consumerism into death, an issue traditionally outside the range of consumer choice.

The main reason why the citizen feels so insecure today is that the *language of security* has been transformed. In western societies, threats have been replaced by risks. When I leave my station every morning I am confronted by a giant information board advising me not to take any 'unnecessary risks' – though what they might be is not stated. In my local supermarket, the customers are issued plastic shopping bags which are 'risk-free'. As well as the perforations that were added some years ago, there is now a clear statement: 'To avoid suffocation keep clear of children' – excellent advice, by the way, whether one is shopping or not.

In the international realm, politics is now the institutionalized attempt to manage the future in the face of unknowable calculations and contradictory certainties. With inter-state conflict displaced from our imagination a transformation of strategic thinking has taken place. At least, during the Cold War, even though we debated intensely and often acrimoniously the difference between Soviet capabilities and intentions, we were able to agree on a military balance based on some form of actuarial accounting: the number of missiles, ships and tanks that made up the threat. Today, there is no actuarial basis for risk assessment. One expert's opinion is no more convincing than another's.

The concept of risk has changed everything, especially the way we conceive of security. Given our understanding that risks, unlike threats, cannot be eliminated, only managed, and that they are neither clear nor quantifiable, the management of risk is inevitably politicized – it is all a matter of subjective understanding. What hope is there for states to agree on the international security environment, when within states this issue is highly politicized as well? Take the debate on the traditionally 'hardest' topic of all – defence against nuclear attack. Back in the early 1990s the US moved from treating the issue as a strategic threat to one of risk management. It went from promising security to its citizens, to promoting enhanced safety of the Russian nuclear arsenal. Security, of course, was necessary in a world in which the Soviet Union might have had the intention to launch a missile strike on the United States. Safety was necessary when there was no such intention on the part of the Russian Federation, but there were very real concerns associated with 'loose nukes', badly maintained nuclear facilities and the possibility of submarine collisions at sea.

Accordingly, in 1995 the US formally abandoned the doctrine of Mutually Assured Destruction (MAD), and opted in its place for the doctrine of Mutually Assured Safety (MAS). Under MAS, a new strategy emerged calling for the de-alerting and de-targeting of missiles. The US also promised to find alternative employment for thousands of nuclear scientists and to help Russia build more secure storage facilities. Yet a few years later, with a new administration in power, MAS was abandoned altogether. Now, the emphasis is on a ballistic missile defence shield. 'Hard' defence is back in fashion, and with it the abrogation of the ABM Treaty, much to the distress of America's European allies.

Discourses on security

None of us should be surprised by the fact that the new language of security has politicized the security debate. Fear has a history and its history is what has changed in recent years. Put another way, security – like everything else – has a historicity.

In his book *Beyond the Pleasure Principle*, Freud divided the history of fear into three eras. That history encompasses every item on today's security agenda. Let me take just one example: disease. In the pre-modern era, people were frightened of disease because they had no explanation for it. It was seen as an act of God or atonement for sin, often vaguely defined. The Black Death which killed off a third of the population of Europe was perhaps the most frightening plague of all because medieval Europeans had no concept of epidemiology.

The modern era, by comparison, was less frightened of disease than it was fearful, especially of the diseases that it recognized spread infection in societies which were becoming increasingly urbanized and integrated. But, at least, its fear was tempered by knowledge of the causes. Indeed, mortality from infection began to decline in the 1850s due to an improvement in social and environmental conditions. The promise of the new age was realized in 1976 with the eradication of smallpox, the first time a disease was eradicated in recorded history.

Our age, as Blinn's novel suggests, is anxious. It is anxious about the return of diseases such as tuberculosis, now highly resistant to drugs. It is anxious about new diseases such as avian flu and their transmission in a globalized age. And it is especially anxious about HIV-AIDS, the subject of four separate UN Security Council meetings which have rendered the pandemic the latest in a long line of social issues to become framed as an international security concern. Now in its third decade, HIV-AIDS is poised to become the most devastating pandemic in world history. Although we have learned more about it in the last twenty years than any other pathogen, there is neither a vaccine nor a cure on the horizon.

Anxiety is factored into the structure of our life. What makes us anxious is that modernity has consequences, or to use a familiar medical metaphor, it has side-effects. And one of the side-effects of diseases such as HIV-AIDS is they have consequences for security – or are at least supposed to. For whether we consider it a security issue at all, will largely be determined by the discourse we conduct with ourselves, a discourse framed by politicians and security experts for their own, often recondite ends. The security environment, to that extent, is something of a cultural construction – a construction of the risk societies we have become.

At the moment, three discourses shape the debate.

1. The World Health Organization prefers to see it as an economic disaster. According to the US Census Bureau's world population profile, 80 per cent of all adult males alive in Botswana today (for its size, one of the richest African countries) may be dead by 2020. Already the life expectancy of the average male has been reduced

from seventy-three ten years ago to thirty-three today. In the Botswana of the future, we may find an echo of Golding's novel *Lord of the Flies*, a world run by twenty-year-olds with little sense of responsibility and no access to the tribal elders, or professional urban expertise.
2. By contrast, the World Bank's recent report *Breaking the Conflict Trap* sees AIDS as part of a larger picture: a crisis in development. Again, this is not surprising if we accept Karl Menninger's observation (quoted by Susan Sontag in her excellent book *Illness as a Metaphor*), 'Illness is only in part what the world has done to a victim; in larger part, it is what the victim has done with his world'. Illness, in other words, is conditioned by lifestyles. Think of the Western obsession with smoking and cancer. It is conditioned also by human habitats (by high urban population growth rates). And it is spread by human action such as global warming, which is becoming especially important in the spread of infectious disease. Illness, in other words, is not merely a matter of biology. It is a matter of social practices. And development agencies are beginning to monitor those practices in order to get funds. Development itself is becoming a strategic tool for conflict resolution, as well as social reconstruction. And development agencies, whether they like it or not – and most do not – are being transformed into security actors in the eyes of many states.

Repackaging security as a development concern brings us back to Gibson's dystopian vision of the future. And to sue a Foucauldian trope – bio-politics – does enhancing our own security involve changing the behaviour of populations within other countries? As a result, are some aspects of policy such as domestic economics, human rights, the status of women, poverty and psychological well-being a matter of international monitoring by Western donor states, aid agencies and NGOs? Is surveillance here, too, the name of the game?
3. The third discourse is a 'hard' security one. For there is no shortage of articles on the impact of HIV-AIDS on international security: studies that argue that the social and political stability of communities, even states, could be undermined by high prevalence rates; concerns raised about the high prevalence rates in African armed forces; and, above all, about the implications for UN peacekeeping.

And the security dimension could be seen to encompass much more than just AIDS. Take malaria – well over a quarter of the US Marines sent into Liberia last year went down with the disease. The lesson – apparently – if you are a terrorist is to hang out in a country with *Plasmodium falciparum* malaria, and recruit locals who have immunity from the disease. Unlikely, but apparently effective.

Criticizing the debate

What I have attempted to discuss in this essay is how we have come to re-perceive the security environment because of the type of societies we have become. The more unpredictable the future becomes, the less inevitable it is. The more accountable it makes us, the more it teaches us that we create it, no-one else, not some divinity or abstract force called Providence. The more it teaches us our responsibility, the more we know that it will be 'other' than we imagine – which is why we read science fiction: the extrapolation of present trends (the present we create) into a future that does not always come to pass. Our actions, in other words, have unintended consequences. The more we accept ourselves as authors of our own fate, of course, the only remaining enigma is ourselves.

But that, as they say, is a question for philosophers...

To conclude, whether we are actually at greater risk than before is not the point: the language of risk is one that encompasses a bewildering set of variables that makes us feel less secure in ourselves, our societies, and even our respective faiths than was true twenty years ago. Anxiety is encoded in our relationship with others. Which is why we have to ask what (for me) is the most important question: how important is the state in determining both our identity and our social relations?

The state is less 'structurally fit' to protect us than we once thought, and globalization has merely highlighted its structural deficiencies. The death, or as Susan Strange would have it, 'retreat', of the nation-state has been so often proclaimed that it is natural, of course, that we should accuse those who go around, lantern in hand like Nietzsche's Madman proclaiming the 'death of God', of 'crying wolf' once too often. But writers such as William Gibson may be on to something. The nation-state was the product of a changing security environment that required what Weber identified as the ultimate mark of the modern state: its monopoly of violence (security under another name). Anxiety now permeates our societies at every level from the local to the global; it often transcends the traditional distinction, encouraging us to think in terms of the 'glocal'. For me, the most challenging feature of our security environment is the decline of the state and the rise of what Ulrich Beck calls a 'feudal, corporative order'. Might we not investigate further his claim that 'the feudal side is not a relic of the past but [is] the foundation and product of industrial society'?

Section 2

Trade Obstacles and Prospects for Growth

Trade, Development and International Institutions: 2005 and Beyond

Razeen Sally

The first few months of 2005 saw a flurry of big, bold initiatives on trade, aid and development, especially with Africa in mind. Meanwhile, President Bush audaciously nominated Paul Wolfowitz to head the World Bank. In Geneva, WTO members are trying to energize Doha Round negotiations in the run-up to the Hong Kong Ministerial Conference in December. Outside Geneva, preferential trade agreement (PTA) initiatives continue to proliferate. Also grabbing headlines is the dramatic opening and global economic integration first of China and now India.

What is one to make of all this? What are the prospects for the Doha Round? What of the WTO's longer-term future? Does the new wave of PTAs bode well or ill for the multilateral trading system? What are the trade (and wider economic and foreign) policy implications of China's and India's integration into world markets? How viable are the new proposals on trade, aid and debt relief? Should 'global governance' be strengthened to tackle these issues? How does all the above fit into the wider framework of international relations post-Cold War and post-11 September?

These are the questions on trade, development and international institutions I address in terms of a 2005 stock-take, and a forward look to medium-term prospects.

Whither the WTO?

The July 2004 negotiating framework has whittled down the Doha Round agenda into one that is better focused. But it is still vague on the key market access issues (agriculture, services and non-agricultural goods); and the tough political decisions lie ahead. My guess is that not much will happen before the Hong Kong Ministerial, and that negotiations will take another couple of years, perhaps more.

What might an eventual deal look like? A big success would deliver substantially lower developed country barriers to developing country exports of agriculture and manufactures, stronger liberalization commitments by advanced developing countries, and some marginal strengthening of WTO rules (e.g., on anti-dumping). As things stand, I think this scenario unlikely. At the other extreme, the round could fail altogether. In between lies modest success: limited liberalization with hardly any rule strengthening. This would keep the WTO show on the road, but it would leave the multilateral trading system in a weak and vulnerable state, increasingly hemmed in by a messy, discriminatory patchwork of PTAs. This is where I would put my money.

Ultimately, bringing the round to a successful conclusion and ensuring the WTO's longer-term relevance depend on tackling its systemic problems. A much expanded post-Uruguay Round agenda has broadened sectoral coverage and gone much deeper into politically sensitive domestic regulation. This has resulted in a loss of focus and a drift towards multiple and contradictory objectives. Hyperinflation of the membership has almost crippled decision-making. The WTO has become much more politicized, buffeted by external criticism and with deep internal fissures. These are all symptoms of the 'UN-ization' of the WTO.

To get the WTO out of its rut, its members need to do two things: restore focus on the core market access agenda – i.e., progressive liberalization; and revive effective decision-making. The latter depends less on reforming formal procedures than on intergovernmental political will and informal decision-making. This requires recognition of hard-boiled realities outside Geneva. About fifty countries account for well over 80 per cent of international trade and foreign investment. This comprises the OECD plus 20-25 developing countries that have been globalizing rapidly and successfully. These are the ones with workable governments, sufficient appreciation of their own interests, negotiating capacity and bargaining power. They must take the lead.

Within this outer core, there is an inner core of 'big beasts': the USA and EU, of course, but now joined by the increasingly influential developing country majors, such as India, China and Brazil. Poorer and weaker developing countries – the vast majority of the membership – must of course be consulted and will exercise influence through the African, LDC, ACP and G90 groupings. But the plain fact is that their very marginal involvement in the world economy, bad-to-terrible governance and scarce negotiating resources make them unable to play more than a secondary and reactive role.

Even with the right dose of realism, there are, in my view, *increasing* limits to WTO-style multilateralism. The GATT was successful because it had (with hindsight) a slim line, relatively simple agenda, and small, club-like decision-making, glued together by Cold War alliance politics. Now, the WTO agenda is technically more complicated, administratively more burdensome and politically much more controversial; decision-making is unwieldy in a general assembly with near-universal membership; and the unifying glue of the Cold War has dissolved.

For the WTO to work after the Doha Round, I think it needs to scale back ambitions and expectations. Market access and rule-making negotiations should be more modest and incremental; and maybe trade rounds should become a thing of the past. There should be more emphasis on the unsexy, everyday tasks of improving policy transparency and administering existing rules better. Dispute settlement should not degenerate into back-door law-making. Finally, core decision-making should remain intergovernmental. Opening it to non-governmental actors would result in an agenda hijacked by organized minorities pursuing a plethora of conflicting objectives.

In sum, with more modest goals and proportionate means in a restricted intergovernmental setting, the WTO might best be able to serve what should be its core purpose: to be, at the margin, a helpful auxiliary to market-based reforms, especially in the developing world.

PTAs as an Alternative?

PTAs among small clubs of like-minded countries can take liberalization and pro-competitive regulatory reform further than would be the case in the WTO. This can in turn stimulate multilateral liberalization. For PTAs to make economic sense, they must have comprehensive sectoral coverage, be consistent with relevant WTO provisions (in Article XXIV GATT and Article V GATS), and indeed go beyond WTO commitments. Liberalization should be genuine and tangible, not bogus. There should be strong provisions for improving transparency in domestic regulation. And rules of origin should be as simple and harmonized as possible to minimize trade diversion and red tape. Overall, governments need to have a sense of economic strategy when entering into PTA negotiations – on choosing negotiating partners, assessing the costs and benefits of negotiating positions, and how they relate to the WTO and to the national economic policy framework.

Unfortunately, strong, WTO-plus PTAs are the exception, not the rule. Most PTAs – especially those between developing countries – are weak and fall short of WTO provisions. They tend to be driven by foreign policy concerns and gesture politics, with little sense of economic strategy. They involve patchy, quick-fix sectoral deals while sensitive areas are carved out. They hardly go beyond WTO commitments, deliver little, if any, net liberalization and pro-competitive regulatory reform, and get tied up in knots of restrictive, overlapping rules of origin. Resource-intensive PTA negotiations also risk diverting political and bureaucratic attention from the WTO and from necessary domestic reforms. Finally, the sway of power politics can result in highly asymmetrical deals, especially when one of the negotiating parties is a major player.

Latin America and Africa now contain a hotchpotch of weak and partial PTAs. This is being replicated in South and East Asia, where PTA initiatives have mushroomed since 1999. Very few of the latter look like delivering strong, clean agreements. The heart of the matter is that cross-border commerce within these regions, as elsewhere in the developing world, is throttled by the protectionist barriers that developing countries erect against their equally poor or even poorer neighbours. Will new PTAs make a big dent in these barriers and thereby spur regional economic integration? I doubt it. To use a 'Texasism', many, perhaps most, PTAs are 'all hat and no cattle'.

Going about PTAs the wrong way – negotiating weak agreements that deflect attention from sensible unilateral reforms and the WTO – could easily lead to a world where most international trade would be governed by a bewildering array of market-distorting preferences. Then the cornerstone of the multilateral trading system, the principle of non-discrimination, would become more an abstraction than concrete reality. That has profound political as well as economic ramifications.

Liberalism From Below and the rise of China and India

It is customary to look first to the WTO, or now to PTAs, or to a combination of the two, to advance the liberalization of international commerce. This 'liberalism from above' overlooks fundamental lessons from theory, history and the world around us today. Compelling political and economic arguments favour *unilateral* liberalization, with governments freeing up international trade and flows of capital and labour independently, not via international negotiations. As any student of trade economics knows, welfare gains result directly from *import* liberalization, which replaces comparatively costly domestic production and reallocates resources more efficiently. Such gains come quicker through own, unconditional liberalization than through protracted, politicized and bureaucratically cumbersome international negotiations. This Nike strategy ('Just Do It') makes political sense too. Rather than relying on one-size-fits-all international blueprints, governments have the flexibility to initiate policies and emulate better practice abroad in experimental, trial-and-error fashion, tailored to specific local conditions.

Observers often forget that the recent trade policy revolution in the developing world has come more 'from below' than 'from above'. The World Bank estimates that, since the 1980s, about two-thirds of developing country trade liberalization has come about unilaterally. True, many governments liberalized reluctantly as part of IMF and World Bank structural adjustment programmes. But the strong and sustained liberalizers have gone ahead under their own steam, without the need for much external pressure.

The big news in globalization today, and probably for the next few decades, is the rise of Asia, and within it the dramatic opening of first China and then India. China's massive trade and investment liberalization programme over the past decade is the biggest the world has ever seen. Most of this was done unilaterally, not through international negotiations, and *before* WTO accession. China's extremely strong WTO commitments, and its very pragmatic, business-like and constructive participation in the WTO since accession, are more the consequence than the cause of its sweeping unilateral reforms.

China is in many ways today what Britain was in the second half of the nineteenth century: the unilateral engine of freer trade. It is probably spurring a pickup in trade and FDI liberalization elsewhere, notably in India. There, market-based reforms since 1991 have proceeded more slowly than in China, but have been very substantial by previous Indian standards. Recently, India has accelerated its unilateral liberalization of tariffs and FDI. Would this have happened, or happened as fast, if China had not concentrated minds? Probably not.

The point I wish to emphasize is this: Freer trade in the early twenty-first century, and modern globalization more generally, are happening more 'from below' than 'from above'. Their engine, now to be found in Asia, particularly in China, is bottom-up liberalization and regulatory reform that spreads through competitive emulation, like ripples and waves across seas and oceans. This process is not driven by international institutions. Indeed, as I have argued earlier, the WTO and FTAs have considerable and perhaps increasing limitations. At best, they can be helpful auxiliaries to national market-based reforms. But their importance should not be exaggerated.

Trade, Aid, Debt Relief, UN Reform: Global Salvationism in the new century

This seems to be the year for grand initiatives on Africa. The biggest and boldest is the UN Report on the Millennium Development Goals, co-ordinated by Jeffrey Sachs. But not far behind are Tony Blair's agenda for the G8 and EU and the Africa Commission Report. All head in the same direction. The Africa Commission Report calls for doubling and possibly tripling aid by 2015, and for the cancellation of all multilateral debt. On trade, it enjoins developed countries to bring down their protectionist barriers in agriculture – e.g., by abolishing trade distorting subsidies to cotton and sugar, offering duty- and quota-free access to all exports from least developed countries, and simplifying rules of origin.

These initiatives are generally commendable for focusing the world's attention on Africa's dire problems. As for the specifics: First, the proposals on trade are wholly welcome. It would be good news indeed if the extra pressure exerted were to goad developed countries to make serious concessions on agriculture in the Doha Round. It has to be said that African countries would gain most if they were to promote further trade and other market-based economic reforms at home, but this should not be a condition for much delayed developed country liberalization. Second, large-scale debt forgiveness is a good idea, but it should be conditional on governments spending the extra resources appropriately. Unconditional debt relief combined with an increase in aid, on the other hand, would be excellent news for more white-elephant projects and presidential Swiss bank accounts. Third, there are welcome noises on making aid transparent, predictable, untied and conditional on good governance in recipient countries.

Now for my scepticism. A half century of aid has been an almost unmitigated disaster. Its politics and psychology are utterly corrupting. It has weaned large, arbitrary and corrupt governments while crowding out markets and individual economic freedom. Hence, a large and sudden increase in aid now is a bad idea for all the old reasons. It will simply overwhelm the supply capacities of already weak and dysfunctional governments. Making it conditional on good governance criteria is wishful thinking. Given the sums and the short timeframe discussed, it is bound to provide more incentives for bigger, wasteful, corrupt and intrusive government. Only the utterly naïve or wilfully disingenuous can aver that good governance will result from aid that accounts for up to two-thirds of government spending and 20-30 per cent of national income (as is proposed in the Sachs Report). True, there is some evidence to show that well-targeted aid can work in better governed countries. But there are very few of these in Africa; and claims made on behalf of some of the 'poster-children', such as Uganda and Tanzania, are too confident and premature – and conveniently suit the interests of those in the aid business.

The failure of the state, not of markets, is central to the African tragedy. A big, aid-induced investment push risks making state failure worse rather than helping to build up viable market societies plugged into the world economy. It is a silly and dangerous idea. The Sachs Report, with its big spending hubris and breathtaking political naivety, should get the Nobel Prize for pottiness and recklessness.

This is not an argument for getting rid of aid altogether. Rather, it would be better to take the existing volume of aid and thoroughly restructure it so that it works better to meet a smaller set of limited, realistic goals. Aid should be redirected from middle-income countries that have good access to capital markets to low-income and especially least developed countries that lack that access. Then it should go to better governed countries, but carefully and gradually according to clearly-defined and well-monitored criteria. There is a case for more aid for specific programmes with clear, precise goals and appropriate mechanisms – e.g., to combat HIV/AIDS and tropical diseases, and meet WTO commitments. Aid should be in the form of grants rather than loans. It should use price-based market mechanisms. And it should bypass governments and deal directly with private organizations on the ground as much as possible.

Underlying these initiatives, especially on aid, is a world view that David Henderson, the former chief economist of the OECD, calls 'Global Salvationism' or 'Deliverance From Above'. It afflicts those who call for stronger global governance. Global solutions are to be provided by concerted co-operation involving governments, international organizations, big business, trades unions and NGOs. The UN system is, of course, front and centre in this scheme. The Sachs Report is suffused with these ideas, as is Kofi Annan's new blueprint for UN reform.

The notion that a global market economy can be planned from

above in this way is profoundly misguided. It is top-down bureaucratic thinking, a sort of soft international central planning for the post-Soviet age. It is Orwellian 'Goodthink' for the twenty-first century. To adapt a 'Bushism', it 'misoverestimates' the importance and effectiveness of international institutions, and 'misunderestimates' their failings, such as self-serving bureaucracy and misguided meddling. Rather successful development, like good trade policy, emerges from below – from national policies and institutions that support markets, and from individuals and enterprises that take advantage of economic freedoms and market incentives. International institutions with limited goals and commensurate means can help at the margin. This, rather than an impossibly ambitious global governance agenda, is what the World Bank, IMF and WTO should promote.

Seen in this light, Paul Wolfowitz's arrival at the World Bank could turn out to be the right and inspired choice, following on the heels of John Bolton's nomination as US ambassador to the UN. Both are political realists who appreciate the power of the USA to provide the global *Pax* and promote a liberal international economic order. Both are sceptics of international organizations and have no time for global governance chatter. Now Wolfowitz should marry his political realism with economic liberalism. The World Bank should promote markets and economic freedom in the developing world, but with more modest, pared-down means and ends. It should emphasize information sharing, the exchange of ideas, policy surveillance and technical assistance. But its power of the purse through project and programme lending should be overhauled and kept within strict limits. And global governance fantasists should be told where to get off.

International Relations: A Post-Cold War, Post-11 September Frame

So far I have placed trade and development in the frame of economic policy; and I have stressed the primacy of national economic policies and institutions. Now it is time to link up to foreign policy and international politics, for this frame is also indispensable for trade and development. A reasonably stable international political order is the categorical imperative for economic development. Without the global *Pax* – an orderly framework for international relations – there can be no security for national and international commerce.

Trade and development must work with the grain of wider geopolitical realities. These have changed since the end of the Cold War, and more recently after 11 September. No serious challenge exists to US leadership abroad; Europe and Japan are internally sclerotic and externally pusillanimous; other powers are on the rise, notably China, India and Brazil; the transatlantic alliance is no longer the fulcrum of international relations; and politics and economics are shifting inexorably in an Asia-Pacific direction.

The one constant in this shifting political template is US leadership. For the foreseeable future, the US will remain the indispensable anchor for global security, prosperity and freedom – far more important than any international organization or international treaty. It is vital that it leads from the front: in securing the global Pax against systemic threats; in helping to rescue and reconstruct failed states; in maintaining open and stable international financial markets; and, not least, in breaking down barriers to trade and the movement of capital and people across the world. Above all, the US must lead by example, setting the standard for liberal economic policies worldwide by what it does at home. This includes untying existing knots of domestic protectionism.

US leadership will be exercised on several tracks: unilaterally; bilaterally and regionally, especially in relations with other powers; and multilaterally through international institutions. Daunting domestic and external obstacles stand in the way of the enlightened exercise of US power and influence abroad. But robust US leadership is *sine qua non* to the future relevance and workability of international institutions such as the WTO, IMF and World Bank. They would be lame and sidelined without it.

Conclusion

To sum up: I am pessimistic about the prospects for a fresh wave of liberalization through the WTO and other international institutions. I think most of the new – or, more accurately, new-old – ideas on aid are wrong. More generally, top-down global-governance prescriptions are profoundly misguided. But I am reasonably optimistic that further liberalization, and with it the spread of economic globalization, will come from a different route: from below through unilateral example setting and competitive emulation. Its engine is China today, and perhaps China plus India the day after tomorrow.

These trade and wider economic policy trends must also be seen in the bigger picture of international politics. Here, the defining features are

US leadership – now more important than ever – and relations between the US and other powers, especially the rising powers in Asia-Pacific, and above all China. International institutions and the transatlantic relationship will matter less, though they are not unimportant.

Overall, this is good news for developing countries with market-based policies and institutions. Going further with liberalization and related regulatory reforms, restructuring the state so that it does fewer things better, widening the space for individuals' economic freedoms – all this will allow countries to take maximum advantage of globalization, raise real incomes, make serious inroads into poverty and generally improve human welfare. This is already happening fast in Asia, but less so elsewhere, and not at all in most of Africa.

The African problem is the failure of the state. The old solutions of aid and policy driven by international organizations, in alliance with venal and thuggish local post-colonial elites, have failed. Short of US-directed liberal imperialism, I am not sure what the solutions are. In any case, the US, unlike Britain in the nineteenth century, is not interested in, and perhaps not capable of, a liberal imperial role in Africa. This leaves a real dilemma.

The WTO and FTAs – an East Asian Perspective

Barry Desker

Introduction

After the debacle of the Seattle World Trade Organization (WTO) Ministerial Conference in December 1999, through to the failure of the Cancun meeting in September 2003, it has become fashionable to speak of the failure, even demise, of the WTO. Such a view has been fuelled primarily by the proliferation of free trade agreements (FTAs) since the late 1990s, particularly the bilateral and regional projects in East Asia. This in itself represents a dramatic shift in the policy preferences of East Asian governments, since for much of the 1970s and 1980s they were staunchly focused on strengthening multilateral institutions such as the GATT and its successor, the WTO. While the current trend towards bilateralism and regionalism can be explained in terms of being a response to the WTO's recent difficulties, it does not explain the shift in policy preferences. Indeed, given that the East Asian economies are largely open economies and reliant on international trade, the fact they have been pushing for FTAs is somewhat counter-intuitive and counter-productive. I will therefore examine the rationale for FTAs in East Asia, from both the perspectives of economic criteria as well as political considerations, and argue that the proliferation of FTAs need not necessarily undermine the WTO system. Indeed, as things stand currently, FTAs, if executed thoughtfully and with the end-game of multilateralism in mind, ought to be seen as a silver lining to the WTO's cloudy prospects.

East Asian FTAs

Standard economic theory holds that open, export-oriented economies should have an interest in maintaining and strengthening the multilateral

---

The author acknowledges the significant assistance of Adrian Kuah, Associate Research Fellow, Institute of Defence and Strategic Studies, in the preparation of this article.

trading system as embodied in the WTO. Furthermore, while the WTO facilitates trade creation, thereby stimulating investment, technology transfer and growth, neoclassical trade theory criticizes FTAs for causing trade diversion, and a net welfare loss. At the institutional level, the multiplicity of rules that result from the proliferation of FTAs convolutes the multilateral trading system that is predicated on the uniformity of rules, such as those governing rules of origin.[1] These reasons, both economic and institutional, suggest that East Asian economies should eschew the FTA strategy, and continue to support the multilateral trade liberalization. The current trends, however, pose a conundrum: If the WTO system is advantageous to East Asian economies, then why the great interest in FTAs so recently?

Critics of FTAs, chief among them prominent economists such as Jagdish Bhagwati and Arvind Panagariya, argue that bilateral and regional trade deals undermine the 'most-favoured nation' (MFN) rule that holds the multilateral system together. Most recently in an article for the *Far Eastern Economic Review* in January 2005, Bhagwati argued that 'the central principle of non-discrimination [the MFN rule: comments mine] has been virtually destroyed... PTAs have proliferated to close to 300 and the number is growing by the week. The agreements which the architects of the GATT thought would be minor exceptions have now swallowed up the trading system'.[2] The burgeoning number of FTAs then leads to a '"spaghetti bowl" problem... characterized by a chaotic criss-crossing of preferences, with a plethora of different trade barriers applying to products depending on which countries they originate from'.[3]

As I have argued elsewhere, I do not disagree with the arguments that Bhagwati *et al.* have levelled against FTAs. However, I would point out that the evidence against FTAs is tenuous at best, and depends very much on what level of analysis is being employed.[4] First, on the issue of trade cre-

---

[1] The WTO's non-discriminatory rules of origin actually favour East Asian economies, because of the nature of their economies: essentially export-oriented manufacturers of products such as semi-conductor components that are produced in various locations along the supply chain.

[2] Jagdish Bhagwati, 'Reshaping the WTO', *Far Eastern Economic Review*, January 2005. What Bhagwati refers to as the 'agreements' are articulated in the so-called enabling clause for FTAs, Article XXIV of GATT, which explicitly stated that the rules did not prevent the formation of FTAs between groups of two or more customs territories.

[3] *Ibid.*

[4] Barry Desker, 'In defence of FTAs: from purity to pragmatism in East Asia', *The Pacific Review* (Vol. 17, No. 1, 2004), pp. 3-26.

ation versus trade diversion, economist Paul Krugman has also argued that the overall welfare effect consists in more than mere trade creation or diversion, arguing that analysis should incorporate whether or not there is a higher degree of competitiveness in each country's domestic production in the wake of joining FTAs. For example, if there is a substitution of uncompetitive domestic production by more competitive imports, then there is a welfare gain; if, however, there is an influx of less competitive imports displacing other imports from outside the FTA, then there is a welfare loss. The picture is certainly more complex than trade creation versus trade diversion.[5]

Needless to say, there are two deeply opposed camps on the issue of FTAs. Those favouring FTAs argue that the name of the game is trade liberalization, regardless of whether it takes place at the multilateral or bilateral level. The argument goes: trade liberalization would have extra-trade impacts such as technology transfer, domestic economic reforms, and growth stimulus effects. Those against FTAs highlight the fact that FTAs are basically a distortion mechanism, and thus constitutes a 'second best' outcome compared to the 'first best' multilateral free trade outcome. FTAs would also create further distortions such as rent-seeking behaviour and the misallocation of resources.

The argument put forward by Bhagwati and Panagariya focus on what is preferable – indeed, there is almost universal consensus that free trade as the end goal, and disregarding for the moment the difficulties involved in getting there, is preferable. However, I believe that an important distinction needs to be drawn between the 'preferable' and the 'possible'. This distinction then enables us to understand why FTAs have proliferated, both in general but particularly in East Asia, and to reconcile the fact of FTA proliferation with East Asian states' continued interest in the multilateral trading system. I would argue that far from being a 'zero-sum' outcome of FTAs undermining the WTO, FTAs would in fact hasten the process of global trade liberalization through incremental, 'bite-size' steps.

---

[5] I argue in the article cited above that other economic variables also affect how one evaluates the welfare effects of FTAs. Some of these include the fostering of competition, market-size effects which affect production patterns, and the impact on the foreign direct investment regime.

FTAs and the Art of the Possible

If politics is the art of the possible, then the phenomenon of East Asian FTA proliferation is pragmatism *par excellence*. As I argued elsewhere, 'while economists may seek the ideal solution, governments will focus on the *politically* attainable, even if it is a second-best choice'.[6] By examining the political rationale for what is essentially an economic decision, one is then able to reconcile how the East Asian economies have been able to negotiate FTAs while still maintaining their broad preference for trade multilateralism. More importantly, one must note the role that exogenous factors – namely, the spectacular failure in Seattle in 1999, and the 1997-98 Asian financial crisis – play in effecting the policy shift towards trade bilateralism and regionalism.

At a more basic level, and prior to these external shocks, the expansion of both the WTO membership and agenda from the mid-1990s led to a slowdown in trade liberalization. Furthermore, the focus on the implementation of the Uruguay Round agreements distracted from further attempts at trade liberalization. These developments led to a gradual disenchantment of East Asian states with the WTO process, and slowly predisposed them towards a more pragmatic approach based on economic regionalism and FTAs. The Seattle episode served to reinforce the East Asian perception that the WTO had become bogged down in terms of internal divisions and had lost its momentum, and that given the lack of progress on global trade liberalization, FTAs would at least contribute by effecting trade liberalization albeit on a smaller scale. Plus, it was politically attainable.[7] At the same time, the financial crisis refocused political energies towards promoting exports growth while causing affected countries to be suspicious and wary towards international organizations. The combination of these *external* factors led to the pragmatic and politically-doable step of bilateral and regional FTAs.

To be sure, the negotiation of FTAs has not been problem-free. The point, however, is that compared to multilateral trade talks, FTAs are easi-

---

[6] Desker, *Op. cit.*, pp. 7-8.

[7] Fred Bergsten, 'Fifty years of the GATT/WTO: lessons from the past for strategies for the future', Working Paper No. 98-3, Institute of International Economics, 1998. Bergsten argues that the momentum of trade liberalization depended very much on the political will that states brought to bear on the process. By the late 1990s, it had become clear that the multilateral process had lost steam, and even regressed, because of the failure to launch a new round in 1999.

er to manage and can be concluded within a much shorter time frame. Furthermore, the fact that the WTO has been overloaded with issues of domestic governance, and tainted by perceptions that double-standards are practiced by powerful members when it comes to the compliance with WTO rules, and the practice of rushed and non-inclusive negotiation sessions, have contributed to the highly protracted process of negotiation, as well as adding to the risk that talks will fail. Simultaneously, these developments serve to fuel ever-greater interest in FTAs. Clearly, FTAs are very much a reality of the international trading system. The question then becomes to what extent FTAs can feed into the WTO system, instead of undermine it?

Given the relative ease with which FTAs can be concluded, East Asian governments will continue to adopt pragmatic albeit 'second best' approaches in the short term, even while maintaining their engagement with the WTO process over the longer term. From a policy perspective, the attraction of the FTA is readily evident: because governments work within four- to five-year electoral cycles, and are governed by the imperatives of performance legitimization, the ability to conclude bilateral and regional FTAs early and smoothly contributes greatly to how governments are assessed by their constituencies. East Asian governments have demonstrated that a parallel track consisting of shorter-term, smaller-scale FTA strategies complementing the longer-term, broader WTO process is possible. Even more importantly, East Asian economic regionalism has shown that far from undermining the WTO process, FTAs have not degenerated into 'closed regionalism' and can play an important part in jump-starting the WTO process. Somewhat tellingly, the World Bank has conceded that FTAs can at least produce some deliverables in the face of WTO stasis. While it is true that the WTO itself has built-in mechanisms to guard against FTAs becoming closed trade blocs, in that FTAs have to be 'WTO plus' agreements, there are in effect no hard and fast guarantees against that happening. What has proven to be instrumental in making this form of parallel track trade diplomacy work has been the pragmatic fusion of two otherwise contradictory notions: the fundamental commitment towards multilateral trade liberalization and the pursuit of FTAs.

Trade Obstacles and Prospects for Growth

Paraschand Hurry

Introduction

There are numerous recent studies on trade obstacles in Africa and the growth prospects of African economies. According to the Blair Commission Report, Africa will fail to achieve sustainable growth and poverty reduction unless it increases its diminishing share of world trade. According to the 2004 WTO World Trade Report, world merchandise trade in 2003 grew by 4.5 per cent in real terms. The most dynamic trading regions were Asia and the transition economies, which had double-digit import and export expansion in their merchandise trade. Import growth in North America exceeded the rate of global expansion and was again much higher than export growth. The volume of merchandise imports went up by 5.7 per cent in the United States, while exports rose somewhat less than 3 per cent, but the latter was the first annual increase after two years of contraction. Western Europe's merchandise exports rose by less than 1 per cent, while imports edged up by nearly 2 per cent. Sustained by a recovery in demand for many primary commodities, Latin America's exports rose by 4.5 per cent, although the region's imports stagnated. Africa as a whole recorded a trade surplus for the first time since 1991, but the continent's share of world exports, 2.3 per cent, was still lower than ten years ago.

Two medium-term developments in international trade are worthy of note. The first is the varied trade performance of different categories of goods and commercial services since 1985. Manufactured goods and other commercial services experienced above average trade growth during this period. By contrast, agricultural and mining products, as well as transport services, saw a relative decline in their trade shares. Secondly, a structural change took place in the composition of world trade in agricultural products, with processed agricultural goods becoming more important. This trend towards more processed goods in trade can be observed across countries and agricultural product groups throughout the 1990-2002 period.

Table 1: World Merchandise Trade by Major Regions, 2003
(Billions of dollars and percentage)

	Exports				Imports			
	Value	% Change			Value	% Change		
	2003	2001	2002	2003	2003	2001	2002	2003
World	7273	-4	4	16	7557	-4	4	16
North America	996	-6	-5	5	1557	-6	2	9
Western Europe	3141	0	6	17	3137	-2	5	3
Africa	173	-6	2	22	165	4	4	17
Middle East	290	-8	1	16	188	5	3	9
Asia	1897	-9	8	17	1734	-7	6	18

Source: WTO Report, 2004

The question of how far trade policy may have been responsible for these observed trends is a matter for further research. This paper discusses briefly obstacles to trade in Africa and seeks to address some measures required for trade to grow. This paper stresses that the contribution of trade policy to growth and development depends largely on a range of related policies.

Brief Overview of Obstacles to Trade in Africa

Despite the many institutional provisions adopted by regional economic groupings with a view to promoting intra-African trade within the various trade agreements which they have signed, official trade between African countries represents a small part of their total trade or tends to remain at the same level. In other groupings (EU, NAFTA, ASEAN, MERCOSUR) intra-regional trade represents the largest part of their international trade. Several factors explain the African exception:

- Barriers to intra-African trade are rooted in the economic structures of the countries; and institutional, infrastructural and financial constraints; financing policies and mechanisms.
- National production profiles do not complement one another since African countries produce and export the same types of products, except for a few countries that have reached a significant level of industrial development. Agricultural and mining products dominate the export structure.

- There is lack of harmonization between regional trade co-operation and national initiatives.
- Despite the efforts undertaken in recent years to improve transport and communications, there are few viable transport and communication channels.
- A number of non-tariff barriers are still applied which pose obstacles to the promotion of intra-Africa trade, like numerous checkpoints, harassment at border points, restrictions on movement of persons.
- Poor banking and financial services also have an impact on trade and productivity. Monetary policies are not harmonized and payments systems are ineffective.
- Other constraints include poor trade marketing, trade information and trade promotion structures.

Need for Policy Coherence

The contribution of trade policy to growth and development depends to a significant extent upon a range of related policies. Well-designed trade policies aimed at gaining maximum advantage from engagement in the international economy can make a key contribution to growth and development. But the value of that contribution is influenced by a number of other policies. There is need for policy coherence in order to create a situation in which relevant policies pull together in a mutually supportive manner.

Policies affecting the macroeconomic environment, infrastructure, the structure of domestic markets and the quality of institutions are important for successful engagement in the international economy.

Macroeconomic Policies

Trade affects the level and composition of activity in the economy, and influences stability and growth. Both exports and imports are determinants of income and employment in the economy. While the causal direction of the relationship between trade and growth has not yet been established, the empirical literature has generally found a positive correlation between the two. Just as trade affects macroeconomic outcomes, changes in national income, employment, the general price level, aggregate investment and consumption also affect trade flows. An expansionary monetary policy and fiscal policy, for example, may be inflationary, affecting the competitiveness of domestic firms with respect to foreign firms. Similarly, an expansionary policy will increase spending, including on imports, and influence the allocation of resources between tradables and non-tradables.

Macroeconomic stability therefore matters for trade. This has been underscored by studies of economic recessions which have pointed to the direct and indirect effects of economic contraction on trade flows. The direct effects come from the decrease in demand for imports when aggregate demand is reduced, while the indirect effects originate in increased pressures from domestic firms for protection against foreign competition. Moreover, increased protection in one country may lead to retaliation and beggar-thy-neighbour responses from other trade partners. This underscores the significant risks for trade occasioned by sharp falls in domestic demand.

Both exchange rate and domestic price stability are strongly correlated with trade performance and external imbalances. Trading partners with low rates of inflation tend to trade more intensively with each other and are more integrated than countries that have experienced greater volatility in the rate of inflation. Counties that experience high exchange rate volatility also tend to be less integrated. Those enduring larger output volatility are also more likely to have lower average trade growth. These results confirm that macroeconomic instability can be detrimental to the growth of trade.

Balance-of-payments imbalances are a reflection of macroeconomic conditions and cannot be effectively addressed through trade policy. The origins of balance-of-payments disequilibrium can vary, and governments must choose between finding ways of financing such imbalances or of adjusting out of them. The choice depends on whether the problem is perceived as temporary or long term. If imbalances reflect longer-term realities, macroeconomic adjustment rather than borrowing is probably needed. Trade restrictions are not effective in solving balance-of-payments problems. Any immediate impact of trade restrictions on the trade balance is likely to be dissipated through shifts in demand from restricted to unrestricted imports and as a result of the harmful effects of import taxes on the cost of export products.

Infrastructure
The effects on trade of the quality, cost and reliability of infrastructure and infrastructural services are far-reaching. Infrastructure and infrastructural

services play a crucial role in supporting the flow of trade. Among key sectors in this regard are transport, telecommunications, financial services and business services. The ability of economic agents to respond to trading opportunities and to compete with imports often depends on the quality, cost and reliability of infrastructure and related services. In addition, the structure of trade will be affected depending on the relative importance of infrastructure and infrastructural services in different economic activities. Sectors that are 'infrastructure-intensive' will be disadvantaged in comparison to those that are not in an environment of inefficient and costly infrastructure and infrastructural services.

Trade Developments in the Common Market for Eastern and Southern Africa (COMESA)

COMESA attained a Free Trade Area in 2000 with eleven participating countries.

Intra-COMESA trade reached US$5.3 billion in 2004 from US$ 3.9 billion in 2000. The trade regime is rules-based, with trade remedy regulations, rules of origin, competition rules, non-tariff barriers reporting mechanisms and trade facilitation instruments.

The trade co-operation is supported with programmes in agriculture, industry, private sector development, communications development and infrastructure.

COMESA also established a programme for macroeconomic convergence for achieving macroeconomic stability. A COMESA Fund is being established with an adjustment facility and an infrastructural fund to assist member states.

COMESA is also working on an Export-Led Strategy to develop the manufacturing sector and increase the export of value added products.

With regard to the multilateral trading system, COMESA has established the Eastern and Southern Africa (ESA) configuration to negotiate the EPAs and is supporting member states in the multilateral trade negotiations in the WTO and greater market access in the developed markets. COMESA is also assisting eligible member states on AGOA.

COMESA is now planning to launch a Customs Union.

Opening to trade in infrastructure services can be an important way of increasing efficiency and competitiveness. Infrastructural services support trade whether or not they themselves are traded. Increasingly, they are tradable and traded, and opening up to trade in these services is one channel through which their quality can be improved and costs reduced. In several of the transport services sectors, market opening can help to create competition in the industry, thereby increasing efficiency. For international transport services to work effectively, a degree of co-ordination is required. This may be partly assured through privately supplied business and logistics services, but international co-ordination of standard setting and trade facilitation also help to reduce costs and transit times for goods and services.

Market Structure, Externalities and Policy Intervention

The full gains from trade liberalization may not accrue to countries if markets are not functioning efficiently. If domestic product markets, or capital and labour markets (factor markets), are functioning poorly, the capacity of economic agents to adjust and take advantage of new trading opportunities will be impaired. The source of market malfunction may relate to anti-competitive behaviour, aspects of government policy or to external factors (externalities) that markets are unable to account for fully. Corrective policies may therefore be required to increase the contestability of markets and address positive and negative externalities.

Competition policies are often needed to secure the gains from liberalization. Competition and trade policies share the objective of promoting competition and achieving efficiency. International trade and investment liberalization increase the competition that domestic producers face from foreigners. In this sense, a small trade-dependent economy with open trade and investment policies may be able to use links with the outside world to ensure competition. But liberal trade and investment regimes are not always enough to secure competitive markets. Other impediments to contestability may necessitate a regulatory response from governments.

Governance and Institutions

The quality of institutions is a primary determinant of how well markets function. The notion of an institution embodies several elements – formal and informal rules of behaviour, ways and means of enforcing these rules, procedures for the mediation of conflicts, sanctions in the case of a breach of the rules, and organizations supporting market transactions. The quality of institutions has long been recognized as an important component of a well-functioning market. The state of institutions will therefore likely affect the amount of trade and welfare generated by trade liberalization. Moreover, the level of social acceptance of trade reform may be affected by a country's institutions.

Well-developed institutions will help to reduce transaction costs for market participants and thus increase the efficiency of markets. If institutions are working effectively, they (i) channel information about market conditions, products and participants; (ii) reduce risk by defining and enforcing property rights and contracts; (iii) circumscribe arbitrary interventions in markets by politicians and interest groups; and (iv) safeguard competition in markets. The availability of information and the assessment of risk are particularly important concerns for foreigners trading with a country. Even if a country lowers its trade barriers, outsiders may be reluctant to trade with the country if, for instance, they do not believe contracts can be enforced or are not sure whether payments will be made.

The quality of institutions is measured by three indicators – government effectiveness, the rule of law and control of corruption. The better the quality of institutions, the greater the difference it makes whether a country has high or low tariffs. If the composite variable used to measure corruption indicates that this problem is sufficiently severe, lower tariffs may have no effect on openness.

Support to Production

The progressive decline of Africa in the share of world trade is partly due to its low capacity to produce and trade competitively in commodities, manufactured products and services. The key problem rests with the 'supply side' of the market. This capacity constraint has been exacerbated by the protectionism facing it in the markets of the developed world and the heavily subsidized developed country exports. The supply side equation is now compounded by the advance the emerging economies have made into world markets, since these economies have established strong competitive advantages. The continent will face even greater challenges as the removal of global trade barriers continue to reduce the value of preferences. Supplies of products also remain heavily dependent on issues mentioned earlier: policy coherence; macro-economic stability; infrastructure; governance; skills; the investment climate; and peace and security.

The Multilateral Trading System

The success of the Doha Round trade negotiations remains vital for maintaining confidence in the multilateral trading system, which is a cornerstone of global economic prosperity. The framework agreement reached in August 2004 has put the Doha Round back on track and both rich and poor countries carry responsibilities for promoting fuller integration of developing countries into the global system.

The implementation of the Economic Partnership Agreements between the EU and ACP countries could lead to a deepening of integration and enhancing intra-African trade, but an unrestricted market access for Africa portends the largest gain for the continent.

Conclusions

The critical challenge to improve the performance of Africa is to open up more to the world. Experience from other parts of the world suggests that non-discriminatory liberalization promotes intra-regional trade as well as with the rest of the world. There is also a need to devote more resources to trade facilitation with focus on reducing bottlenecks and impediments to trade. International organizations like the IMF and the World Bank should strengthen co-operation and technical assistance in managing shocks from trade liberalization and integration. Above all, our countries need to demonstrate strong commitment to trade reform to reverse the current situation.

Promoting African Trade: Issues, Prospects and Challenges

Mills Soko

Three interconnected arguments are advanced in this paper. The first is that although trade can undoubtedly play an important role in facilitating the integration of the African continent into the global economy and in reversing its subordinate role in world trade, not all African countries will benefit from a liberalized global trade regime. In particular, with a few exceptions, trade liberalization is likely to have adverse effects on the least developed countries (LDCs). The international community has an obligation to implement compensation and adjustment programmes to ensure that these countries can cope with liberalization.

The second contention is that domestic policies are as equally important as international policies in addressing Africa's trade concerns. If trade is to work for Africa, it is necessary that African countries accord the same rigorous attention to the reorientation of their domestic policies as they do to the reform of international policies.

The third is that while trade can contribute toward African economic recovery, it is not a panacea for the complex and multi-dimensional development problems of the continent. There should also be greater concentration on strengthening other policies, such as investment policy, research and development policy, technology policy and skills development policy.

Departing from the premise that Africa's precarious and marginal position in the contemporary world economy is the consequence of the interplay of external and internal factors, the following section discusses some policy interventions that ought to be undertaken by African countries and the international community to promote African trade and to ensure that the continent meaningfully exploits the benefits of trade. Specific focus is placed on the following areas: agriculture; market access; LDC concerns; intra-regional integration; production and export diversification; and domestic policies.

Reviving Agriculture

Agriculture is the cornerstone of African economies and the key to the continent's economic revival. Apart from making up 35 per cent of Africa's gross domestic product, it accounts for 70 per cent of the region's employment and 40 per cent of its exports. Yet, in spite of the preponderance of its agricultural sector, Africa is the only region where per capita food self-sufficiency has decreased considerably, dropping by 12 per cent between 1961 and 1995.[1]

If Africa is to attain food security and self-sufficiency, government policies must undergo substantial change. The failure of African governments to undertake appropriate agricultural domestic reforms over the past decades has contributed immensely to the continent's dreadful agricultural performance.

The principal challenge is to eliminate gender inequalities in rural development policies. Women constitute the bedrock of agricultural production in Africa. Even so, they are still confronted with daunting problems of access to land, credit, education and health care. There is a need to make women active partners in the development process not only by involving them in the design and implementation of mainstream agricultural programmes, but also by ensuring equitable access to credit, income distribution and land reform.[2]

Africa must also overcome its serious infrastructural weaknesses. Efforts must be directed at developing an infrastructure that ensures a safe and efficient production, processing, and transportation of food within and between countries, especially between Africa's food surplus and food deficit nations. Moreover, there is a need to establish effective marketing and storage systems, which are essential to the long-term viability of African farming; it is estimated that close to 40 per cent of African crops are lost to deficient transport and storage.[3]

Africa's environmental problems have undermined the continent's agricultural productivity. Deforestation, soil erosion and low productivity have conspired to undermine Africa's agricultural development. Policies

---

[1] Fantu Cheru, *African Renaissance – Roadmaps to the Challenge of Globalisation* (London: Zed Books, 2002), p. 89.
[2] See Katrine Saito, Hailu Mekonnen and Daphe Spurling, 'Raising the Productivity of Women Farmers in Sub-Saharan Africa,' World Bank Discussion Paper No. 230, Washington, DC, 1994.
[3] Cheru, *op cit*., p. 116.

that encourage environmentally sustainable, productive agricultural practices are required.

Erstwhile initiatives to bolster African agriculture have been marred by excessive state interference. Inept and misguided macroeconomic and trade policies aggravated food insecurity in numerous African countries. While African states have an important role to play in advancing rural development, they should promote policies that allow private enterprise to: improve the quality of products; help small farmers acquire knowledge and land, and a better legal framework for land titles; purchase seed, fertilizer and equipment; gain access to markets; and remain competitive as markets become more open.[4]

The international community has a vital role to play in fostering agricultural development in low-income countries. As stated in the Doha Declaration, the effective implementation of capacity building in developing countries is crucial. Investment should be directed towards: the installation of appropriate food production and processing capacity and technologies; education and training, particularly in technical areas such as sustainable agriculture, quality control and packaging; the development of necessary infrastructure, such as finance, distribution, irrigation with a responsible use of water and communication systems; institution building, in the form of land titles, research centres, regulatory and food safety assurance bodies.[5]

The agricultural sector has the potential to secure food self-sufficiency, expand economic opportunities for growth, and propel industrialization and social progress across Africa.

Widening Market Access

Widening access for competitive African exports, especially agriculture, to developed country markets is central to advancing African trade. Yet any attempt to address Africa's agricultural concerns cannot ignore the issue of agricultural subsidies in the developed countries. High agricultural subsidy support in the industrialized countries considerably damages the economies of poor countries, the majority of which are African. Dismantling trade barriers is, therefore, central to the economic rejuvena-

---

[4] International Chamber of Commerce, *Policy Statement – Agricultural Trade and the Doha Development Agenda*, November 18, 2002, p. 5.
[5] World Trade Organisation, *Doha Declarations,* Geneva, 2002.

tion of Africa: It would enhance agricultural production in countries where food could be produced most efficiently and in a more sustainable fashion, especially in those countries faced with endemic food insecurity.

Research done by the World Bank shows that eliminating trade distortions has the potential to considerably increase real incomes and reduce poverty in poor countries. It is estimated that the total benefit of liberalizing agricultural trade globally will be in the region of US$250 billion by 2015, with US$150 billion accruing to developing countries.[6] For these reasons, it is imperative for industrialized countries to radically overhaul their agricultural policies, especially with regard to the elimination of market-distorting export subsidies, export credits and direct payments, as well as market access restrictions – particularly tariff escalation and tariff peaks.

The drive to broaden market access must also take into account the needs of African clothing and textile producers. This is important in light of the recent significant changes to the global textile trade regime, typified by the emergence of China as the world's most competitive textile manufacturer.

Addressing LDC concerns

Capacity constraints have severely hampered the ability of the LDCs to participate effectively in and cope with the obligations imposed by the World Trade Organization (WTO). There is a direct link between the issues of technical assistance and market access: even if the LDCs are granted access to industrialized country markets, their supply-side constraints bar them from taking full advantage of these market openings. Improved technical assistance could play a vital role, therefore, in reinforcing the ability of developing nations to assess the advantages and costs of various trade agreements and enabling them to participate more effectively in trade negotiations and dispute settlement.

In line with the Doha mandate, technical assistance must also be extended to the LDCs in the area of trade facilitation. This is crucial to improving the management of cross-border trade and distribution of goods, and to simplifying customs procedures, thereby reducing losses suffered by businesses through unnecessary delays at borders.

The value and impact of regional and bilateral trade agreements

---

[6] World Bank, *Global Economic Prospects and the Developing Countries 2003: Investing to Unlock Global Opportunities*, Washington, DC, 2003.

between the LDCs and industrialized countries needs to be assessed. In a 2005 report, the World Bank warned poor countries against rushing into trade deals with developed countries and pointed out that poorly conceived trade deals would result in diminishing returns – or even economic losses – for the LDCs.[7]

But it is also important to recognize that not all the LDCs will benefit from trade liberalization. Studies show that, with a few exceptions such as cotton producers, trade liberalization may have unintended adverse effects on the LDCs. The international community – notably multilateral agencies such as the World Bank and the International Monetary Fund – has a responsibility to ensure that appropriate compensation and adjustment programmes are designed for countries that are likely to be harmed by liberalization.

Promoting Intra-regional Integration

The regionalization of the world economy has reinforced the vulnerability of Africa in the international economy and underscored the centrality of intra-regional integration to the continent's development. Pressing demands for globalization, coupled with the economic setbacks of the past two decades, have exposed the futility of pursuing nationalistic development in Africa.

Yet the record of regional economic integration in Africa has been one of unmitigated failure. Sub-Saharan Africa is replete with over-ambitious, grandiose and overlapping regional integration plans that have failed to materialize. Intra-regional trade in Africa is severely constrained by a plethora of structural factors including the lack of adequate transport and communications infrastructure, the poor implementation of regional trade agreements, the absence of complementarity in production, as well as weak financial sectors. The failure of regionalism in Africa has been reflected predominantly in the low levels of intra-regional trade – for instance, in 2000 only 2 per cent of African cross-border trade occurred among African states.[8]

Strengthening regional and sub-regional integration among African states is thus necessary if they are to reverse their marginalization in world trade.

---

[7] *World Bank, Global Economic Prospects: Trade, Regionalism and Development,* Washington, DC, 2005.

[8] Hawkins, T, 'Africa Trade,' Policy Brief – The Evian Group, Lausanne, 2002.

Diversifying Production and Exports

A striking feature of African economies today – more than twenty years after the 'lost decade' of the 1980s – is their unchanged terms of incorporation into the international division of labour: They remain locked into the role of traditional commodity exporter and importer of capital goods and technologies. Their disarticulation from the global economy is exemplified by the serious deficiencies that characterize their foreign trade. African economies rely excessively on slow growth commodity exports. While East Asian countries succeeded over the past decades to diversify their exports and transform themselves into internationally competitive manufacturing economies, their African counterparts have lagged far behind. Closely tied to high export dependence is the problem of product concentration. Most African economies are undiversified and exports are concentrated in a narrow range of products. Primary commodities still account for about 70 per cent of exports from Sub-Saharan Africa.[9]

With the exception of a few countries such as South Africa, Morocco and Mauritius – which have a relatively diversified export base – African external trade continues to revolve around one or two traditional commodities, mainly oil and agricultural exports. This renders African economies vulnerable to external shocks such as volatile swings in commodity prices, which have an adverse impact on their terms of trade and overall growth. Indeed, export instability has been the key factor responsible for chronic current account deficits and balance of payments crises in African countries.

Diversifying Africa's production and exports is vital to the overall success of their trade performance. African countries must eschew their excessive dependence on commodity exports and develop import and export policies that will foster industrialization and serve as sources of innovation in the economy. The urgency of carrying out the necessary policy, institutional and administrative reforms to achieve these ends cannot be over-emphasized.

Reforming Domestic Policies

The experience of numerous countries in Sub-Saharan Africa in the 1970s demonstrated unequivocally that a positive international economic envi-

---

[9] World Bank, *Global Development Finance*, Washington, DC, 2002.

ronment was not sufficient to guarantee self-sustained growth. The investment and growth generated by African countries was not accompanied by efforts to raise domestic savings and diversify exports. This meant that when the external economic environment weakened, African growth could not be sustained. Aligning domestic actions with international policy efforts remains, therefore, a key imperative for African governments. To this end, concerted efforts must be made to undertake appropriate reforms in domestic policy areas including savings and investments, exchange rates, education and training, research and development, technology development, as well as political and economic institutions.

The failure by African countries to generate sufficient levels of foreign direct investment has underscored the importance of generating internal resources for Africa's social and economic advancement. Without substantial domestic savings and investment, African states will not be able to build a sound public and social infrastructure and tackle the monumental developmental challenges they confront. National savings and investment played a crucial catalytic role in the successes of the East Asian economic tigers, where the saving ratio in most countries was estimated at 50 per cent compared with 18 per cent in Africa. A major problem is that 33 per cent of Africans' savings are held offshore, thanks to anxieties about political and economic instability in many parts of the continent.[10] Creating a political and economic climate conducive to local investment is thus a key test for African governments. African governments would be better served if they also tapped into the enormous internal investments that are locked in the 'informal sector', which could contribute considerably towards evolving alternative strategies of accumulation.

Tied to this is the need to recognize the growing nexus between international migration and development. In particular, African countries must develop innovative ways in which migrant remittances can be used to finance African development. According to the World Bank, Africa receives 15 per cent of total remittances (estimated at $80 billion in 2002) to the poor countries.[11]

---

[10] Bade Onimode, *Africa in the World of the 21st Century* (Ibadan: Ibadan University Press, 2000), p.234.

[11] Cerstin Sander and Samuel Maimbo, 'Migrant Labour Remittances in Africa – Reducing Obstacles to Developmental Contributions,' *Africa Region Working Paper Series* No.64, World Bank, Washington, DC, November 2003.

Policy reforms must also tackle the problems that stifle entrepreneurship development. Too many businesses in Africa operate in the informal economy, without the necessary institutional support. Weak financial systems, insufficient transport and communications infrastructure, a lack of protection for property rights, and the absence of dispute settlement mechanisms for private parties are some of the problems that militate against the emergence of a vibrant entrepreneurial culture. A dynamic private sector can contribute significantly not only to poverty reduction, but also to the development of entrepreneurial skills and expertise. Through better access to information technology and telecommunications, it can also enable businesses to access global markets through integrated supply chains.

Any attempts to reverse Africa's marginalization in the global political economy will not succeed unless they simultaneously address the crisis of governance in the region. Economic crises in Africa have engendered political and social crises and collectively they have propelled the downward spiral in the majority of countries. Combined with the absence of democratic accountability, the paucity of visionary leadership in Africa has been a major contributor to its multifarious socio-economic and political ills. Although Africa has made remarkable strides towards embracing democracy over the past decade, autocratic and self-serving rule continues to be a defining feature of politics in many parts of the region. African leaders cannot claim to be active champions for reform in global economic governance while domestically induced problems of political misrule, endemic corruption, human rights abuses, high levels of capital flight and gross fiscal mismanagement continue to linger on unchecked.

The Future for Regional Integration in sub-Saharan Africa

Richard Gibb

Regional integration is widely regarded as a policy capable of lessening Africa's economic and political marginality. The creation of a continental African common market by 2025 is the cornerstone of the Abuja Treaty, adopted by the Organization of African Unity (OAU) in 1991 and subsequently by the African Union (AU). The New Partnership for Africa's Development (Nepad) also prioritizes the creation of regional common markets as a mechanism to integrate Africa more effectively in the global economy. With a few notable exceptions,[1] there is a remarkable degree of consensus that regionalism is not only desirable but also necessary. The conclusion to the 1994 African Development Bank study on economic integration concludes that 'regional integration is not an optional extra; it is a matter of survival'.[2] However, the continent already has a large number of regional blocs (fourteen in 2004) with increasingly ambitious policy gaols, centred primarily on the creation of regional common markets. In fact, the region is host to the oldest customs union in the world, the Southern African Customs Union (SACU), which predates the European Economic Community (EEC) by almost forty years. In short, regional integration is a fashionable but far from novel phenomenon in sub-Saharan Africa.[3]

The central contention of this paper is that whilst regional integration has the potential to contribute positively to the trade, development and security relationship, regionalism by itself is just one component of a whole suite of reforms needed to lessen Africa's marginality. It is certainly

---

[1] See Jeffrey Herbst, 'Developing nations, regional integration and globalism', paper presented to a conference 'South Africa and Southern Africa, 16-17 July 1997, South African Institute of International Affairs, Johannesburg.
[2] African Development Bank (1993) Economic Integration in Southern Africa, Volumes I, II, III, Biddles, England, p. 1.
[3] Andrea Goldstein, The new regionalism in sub-Saharan Africa, *Policy Brief* No. 20 (Paris: OECD, 2002).

not a panacea for Africa's problems.

Regional integration can only really be as strong as its constituent parts or as strong as its constituent parts want it to be. The problem in sub-Saharan Africa is, not surprisingly, the strength, or more precisely the weakness, of the constituent parts (the states). With a few notable exceptions, the states are generally weak and, in certain cases, dysfunctional. Two of the most important regional institutions within sub-Saharan Africa, the Southern African Development Community (SADC) and the Common Market for Eastern and Southern Africa (COMESA), are undermined by the existence (and indeed persistence) of weak or dysfunctional states. In the case of SADC, the Democratic Republic of Congo, Angola and, to a lesser extent, Zimbabwe serve to undermine the cause of regionalism. In the case of COMESA, the list of weak/dysfunctional states is even longer: Angola, Burundi, DR Congo, Rwanda, Sudan, Ethiopia and Zimbabwe. Sub-Saharan Africa's record of creating and sustaining effectively functioning regional frameworks is hence generally very poor.[4] Why?

Regionalism: The Economic Rationale

Geographically, the appeal of regionalism in sub-Saharan Africa is almost intuitive. For example, the fourteen countries belonging to SADC (Table 1), despite having a combined population of over 205 million, represent a small and peripheral component of the world economy, with a combined GDP of US$164 billion (roughly equal to that of Poland's). Clearly, the individual countries of southern Africa, including South Africa, are marginal players in global trade. According to the World Trade Organization,[5] the whole of Africa accounts for just 2.1 per cent of merchandise exports and 2.5 per cent of merchandise imports.

Regional integration is widely perceived as a powerful instrument to combat this 'peripherality' and promote economic development. Extreme geographical fragmentation combined with the problems of economic/political survival has encouraged the formation of a large number of inter-state organizations and institutions. Theoretically, by joining together, states are in a better position to exploit larger scale economies

---

[4] Ibid.

[5] WTO (2004) Annual Report, Volumes I and II, The World Trade Organization, Geneva.

and, at the same time, restructure the regional economy in a way that benefits the production base of the region. It is also seen as a way to reduce the exploitative dependency relationships arising from limited and unspecialized internal markets. This economic rationale explains why the creation of trading blocs has been, and continues to be, at the very centre of intra-African co-operation.[6]

Regionalism is also seen as a mechanism to integrate more successfully into the global economy. In 2000, the executive president of the SADC, Prega Ramsamy, argued for greater regional integration on the grounds that:

> *[the] individual economies of most member states are not internationally viable and competitive, as they are not in a position to enjoy the required economies of scale and to effectively deal with constraints to international competitiveness.*[7]

Given the small size of the region's economy, its peripherality in the world trading system and pressures emanating from the world economy, particularly liberalization as manifested through structural adjustment programmes and international trading agreements like the Uruguay Round and Cotonou, regional economic integration is seen as a means of survival in a rapidly globalizing era:

> *Regional integration will prepare us for global competition. If we do not integrate now and put our industries on a more competitive basis, they will be wiped out...*[8]

Notwithstanding the widespread support for regional economic integration, there are several issues that serve to undermine the economic rationale supporting African regionalism. First, despite the existence of a myriad of regional trading blocs, intra-African trade remains limited for the majority of African states. With the exception of the SACU, regional trading blocs have failed to achieve any significant integration in merchandise goods markets. Intra-African trade remains a small fraction of each

---

[6] Charles Harvey, 'The role of Africa in the global economy: the contribution of regional co-operation, with particular reference to Southern Africa', BIDPA working paper no. 11, Gaborone, 1997.

[7] Prega Ramsamy, 'Poverty Reduction: A top priority in SADC's integration agenda', SADC Review, (SADC, Gaborone, 2000), p. 3.

[8] Joachim Chissano, 'Official SADC Trade, Industry and Investment Review', *SADC Review* (SADC, Gaborone, 2000).

country's total commerce.⁹ In the case of SADC, intra-regional trade stood at approximately 6 per cent in 2003. This compares unfavourably to most other trading blocs (Table 2). Furthermore, trade as a percentage of GDP is usually not more than 25 per cent. The impact of regional integration on trade and development is, therefore, likely to be small in the aggregate. Regional trade represents 3 to 4 per cent of GDP. The lack of complementarity between integrating states is one of the principal reasons explaining the limited impact of regionalism on promoting trade and development in sub-Saharan Africa. In short, the trade effects from regional integration will, for the foreseeable future, be small.

Second, as outlined above, most sub-Saharan economies are small and marginal players in global trade. A united Africa would not be a major economic force. It is a sobering thought that the combined African economy, including South Africa, would be smaller then that of the Benelux! This led Jeffery Herbst[10] to ask the rather blunt question: 'Why go through the effort to try to have a relatively small number of extraordinarily poor people trade with each other when the world economy is larger, more populous, and growing faster?' There are, of course, many answers to that question, not least the disadvantageous terms of trade between Africa and the industrialized 'North'. Nonetheless, Herbst's question serves to highlight that the trade effects from African integration will be small and that the greatest potential for growth rests with engaging more successfully in the global economy. With the exception of SACU, the economy-led approach to regional integration in Africa has failed to promote substantial progress in trade or development. Herbert observes that:

> *Africa has embraced the questionable notion that everything should be resolved through regional solutions... They pretend to be development agencies when they fundamentally can do no more than convene meetings and facilitate.*[11]

This failure has been reinforced by the impact of structural adjustment policies on the ability of governments to manage their economies. The agenda introduced by so-called 'new regionalism', based on the free movement of services, capital and attracting FDI, is likely to face the same

---

⁹ Goldstein, *Op. cit.*

[10] Herbst, *Op. cit.*

[11] Ross Herbert, 'Building blocs: are regions the answer?', *eafrica* (Johannesburg: South African Institute of International Affairs, Vol. 2. 2004), p. 1.

impediments as the old economy-led approach: namely, a lack of complementarity between member states.

To a certain extent, the economic rationale supporting regional integration amongst African states fell foul of what Goldstein refers to as a 'fallacy of transposition',[12] assuming that the experience of regional integration in Europe could be replicated in Africa. Clapham observes that:

> *African regional integration schemes have been established in terms of a completely misconceived analogy with the European Union, in terms of which a process of progressively closer economic integration was (at least rhetorically) expected to lead to the political union implicit in the Pan-African project.*[13]

However, European integration was, and to a large extent still is, driven by political and security issues, rather then trade and economic development issues. In most cases, however, the two are inter-related. And throughout Africa, the political issues of security, development and good governance are gaining in significance as the economy-led approach to integration becomes increasingly discredited.

Regionalism: The Political Rationale

Regional integration has a potentially important role to play in promoting peace and security. The classical liberal argument is that greater economic interdependence reduces conflict and enhances security. In theory, by providing an institutional rules-based framework for trade, regional integration promotes greater security. However, this theory only works when regional integration stimulates intra-regional trade and promotes economic interdependence. Both of these assumptions have been questioned. Furthermore, when intra-regional trade does take place, it often does so in a geographically uneven way, promoting rivalries between 'winners' and 'losers'.

Instead of promoting trade that creates security, perhaps regional integration could be better focused on promoting peace and security, and,

---

[12] Goldstein, *Op. cit.*, p. 6.
[13] Christopher Clapham, 'The changing world of regional integration in Africa', in Christopher Clapham, Greg Mills, Anna Morner, and Elizabeth Sidiropoulos (eds), *Regional Integration in Southern Africa* (Johannesburg: South African Institute of International Affairs, 2001), p. 59.

in so doing, helping to create conditions suitable for trade. In a review of African integration, Clapham argues that 'where regional economic organisations did have any significant impact on regional relationships, this was much more likely to be in the field of security than that of economic development'.[14] Both Ecowas and SADC have intervened to secure regional peace settlements, most notably in Liberia and Lesotho, respectively. However, the success of these interventions is often questionable, producing significant regional tensions. Furthermore, as observed by Mbeki, during the past fifty years there has been an almost complete absence of African inter-state wars:

> ...there have only been three inter-state wars among African countries: between Tanzania and Uganda in the 1970s; between Ethiopia and Eritrea in the 1990s; and amongst several states and non-state belligerents in the Democratic Republic of Congo.[15]

Africa's security problems are concerned less with inter-state conflict than national issues of good governance and representative, accountable government. Although these are traditionally perceived of as 'national' issues, bad governance has regional repercussions, both economic and political. If regional integration could be used to promote good governance, accountability and transparency, and 'lock-in' national reforms to a regional agenda, it has the ability to create the conditions for the private sector to promote trade and development.

Conclusion

Regional trade and regional security, development and peace, are heavily inter-linked and related to the condition of the African state. As noted at the beginning of this chapter, regionalism can only be as strong as its constituent parts. Without good governance – both at the national and regional scale – the gains from regional integration will be limited. If regional integration promotes good governance, peace and stability, it will promote trade and development. Thus far, regional integration has not been used effectively to promote good governance.

---

[14] Clapham, *Op. cit.*, p. 62.
[15] Moeletsi Mbeki, 'regionalisation and Africa's search for economic renewal', *eafrica* (Johannesburg: South African Institute of International Affairs, Vol.2, 2004), p. 5.

Tswalu 2005

Table One: Selected socio-economic indicators, SACU Member States, 2001/02

Country	Population (millions) 2002	GDP* (US$Billion) 2002	GNI** Per Capita US$ 2002	Net Foreign Assets Billions of national currency 2002	Merchandise Exports (f.o.b) US$ millions	Merchandise Imports (f.o.b) US$2002	Energy Production (KTO11 equivalent*** 2001
Angola	13.12	11248	670	94	8343	3709	43559
Botswana	1.71	5273	3010	31	2279	1596	0
Burundi	7.07	719	100	18	48	115	0
Comoros	0.59	247	390	39	19	45	0
Congo (DRC)	51.58	5707	90	-222	1088	1061	15707
Djibouti	0.69	553***	900	47	72***	271***	0
Egypt	66.37	90650	1470	19	7005	17411	59301
Eritrea	4.3	642	180	1	54	520	0
Ethiopia	67.22	6059	100	11	431	1696	18000
Kenya	31.35	12330	360	107	2169	3058	12644
Lesotho	1.78	714	470	4	373	796	0
Madagascar	16.44	4400	230	2194	499	620	0
Malawi	10.74	1901	160	4	421	727	0
Mauritius	1.21	4533	3900	44	1569	1799	0
Mozambique	18.44	3599	210	12150	682	1263	7560
Namibia	1.99	2904	1960	2	1205	1368	294
Rwanda	8.16	1732	210	103	67	234	0
Seychelles	0.08	699	7050	0	236	376	0
South Africa	45.35	104242	2600	75	32042	27556	145287
Sudan	32.79	13516	380	-626	1948	2153	21551
Swaziland	1.09	1186	1240	3	957	1037	0
Tanzania	35.18	9382	290	1169	903	1514	13001
Uganda	24.6	5803	240	1553	474	1066	0
Zambia	10.24	3697	310***	-2599	916	1204	6052
Zimbabwe	13	8304	450***	-12	1730	1413	8531

* Gross Domestic Product, real. Millions of US dollars (current 1995 prices)
** Gross National Income per capita. Atlas Method (World Bank, 2004, 38)
*** Energy production refers to commercial forms of primary energy converted into oil equivalents (world Bank, 2004, 257)

To a large extent, the regional institutions of southern Africa – SACU, SADC, COMESA and the EAC – are focused almost entirely on trade issues and the creation of customs unions. However, formal inter-state regional economic integration agreements are unlikely to be beneficial (by themselves) to the countries of sub-Saharan Africa in the foreseeable future.[16] The countries of sub-Saharan Africa have few of the characteristics associated with successful regional integration movements. Bluntly put, sub-Saharan Africa is too small and weak to sustain itself through increased intra-regional trade. That said, given the extreme geographical segmentation of sub-Saharan Africa and the economic vulnerability of many states, regional integration, both economic and political, will help determine the future of this continent. It needs to focus on political as well as trade issues, promoting peace and security through good governance.

Regionalism has an important role to play in determining Africa's future. But it needs to address domestic as well as international issues, political as well as trade issues, peace as well as development. In short, the challenges facing African regionalism are the same as those facing the African state.

Table Two: The regional share (per cent) of trade

	Intra-regional exports as share of total (2003, or last year available)	Intra-regional imports as share of total (2003, or last year available)
EU (15)	61.6	61.9
NAFTA	56.5	38.1
ASEAN (10)	24.0	23.6
MERCOSUR	11.5	17.0
ANDEAN	10.2	13.9
CARICOM	9.8	16.4
COMESA	8.6	5.8
SADC	6.0	6.3

Source: IMF, ODI, LM

---

[16] Steven Radelet, 'Regional integration and co-operation in sub-Saharan Africa: are formal trade agreements the right strategy?', Africa Economic Policy Paper no.20, Washington, 1999.

Section 3

'Goods and 'Bads': Obstacles for African Stability and Security

Governance in sub-Saharan Africa: Building the Foundation for Prosperity and Security

Jeffrey Herbst

While there are no magic bullets for Africa, it is now widely recognized that governance – reasonably defined by the World Bank as 'the traditions and institutions by which authority in a country is exercised for the common good'[1] – is central to the stability of African countries and their ability to prosper in the international economy. African countries that have institutions that enforce property rights, promote accountability in government, and allow for integration in the global economy are more likely to have higher levels of growth than others who perform less impressively on these dimensions. Those countries with higher governance levels are also likely to be more secure because institutions will be accountable to the views of citizens and more will believe that the way to greater riches is through normal commerce rather than resorting to violence. Mechanisms for conflict resolution amongst different groups are also more likely to work in countries with relatively well-functioning governance institutions.

The virtues of governance are more or less universally acknowledged. This paper examines governance trends in sub-Saharan Africa to better understand the current state of governance and to suggest what different African countries will have to do in order to reap the fruits of good governance in the future. In particular, the paper attempts to go beyond the now ritualistic acknowledgement of Africa's diversity and

---

[1] The full definition used by the Bank is: the traditions and institutions by which authority in a country is exercised for the common good. This includes (i) the process by which those in authority are selected, monitored and replaced, (ii) the capacity of the government to effectively manage its resources and implement sound policies, and (iii) the respect of citizens and the state for the institutions that govern economic and social interactions among them. See:
http://www.worldbank.org/wbi/governance/about.html. Viewed on 25 March 2005.

tries to group countries according to the very different governance challenges they face.[2]

African Governance in Comparative Perspective

There are many ways to measure governance – none perfect – although given how closely related different measures are to each other, most tend to tell the same general story, even if ranking countries somewhat differently. The World Bank has developed a measure of 'government effectiveness' that 'combines responses on the quality of public service provision, the quality of the bureaucracy, the competence of civil servants, the independence of the civil service from political pressures, and the credibility of the government's commitment to policies'.[3] Far more complicated statistical exercises are possible, although the value added of such attempts are limited and 'governmental effectiveness' certainly goes to the core of many governance issues. The Bank has estimated government effectiveness for most countries in the world and centred the average at 'zero'. That is, the 'average' country has a government effectiveness rating of zero, with those below average having negative ratings.

While all measures of governance need to be treated carefully, it is important to measure the absolute measure of governance in a country. The recent Millennium Project report to the UN Secretary-General argued that governance in African countries was important but had to be viewed accounting for current levels of income. Thus, Central African Republic, Côte d'Ivoire, Nigeria and Togo were given 'average' scores for governance because they had both low governance scores and low per capita income.[4] The problem with this argument is that investors do not ask if governance is appropriate for the income level of a country, they ask if they can get their contracts enforced in a reasonable period of time. Similarly, those

---

[2] For instance, the recent Commission for Africa report notes Africa's diversity but does not try to differentiate countries according to governance performance, even while stressing the need for greater governance. Commission for Africa, *Our Common Interest: Report of the Commission for Africa*, March 2005.

[3] Daniel Kaufmann, Aart Kraay and Masssimo Mastruzzi, 'Governance Matters III: Governance Indicators for 1996-2202,' April 5, 2004, p.3. Found at: http://www.worldbank.org/wbi/governance/pdf/govmatters3_wber.pdf. Viewed 28 March 2005.

[4] Millennium Project *Investing in Development: A Practical Guide to Achieve the Milllennium Development Goals* (London: Earthscan, 2005), p. 147.

groups deciding on whether to resort to violence in order to achieve their political means do not assuage themselves by noting that their countries' governance measures are adequate considering their level of income. Using the Millennium Project's approach, a country's governance scores might go up if its national income suddenly went down due to a natural disaster, making it an interesting statistical approach but not one attuned to the demands of citizens.

There are obviously significant margins of errors in any measure of governance, as there is only limited information on how many governments function and some categories are inherently hard to measure. Thus, in the following table, it would be inappropriate to assert that Ghana actually has better governmental effectiveness than Seychelles because it has a score that is 0.01 higher. It would be reasonable to assert that Ghanaian government is probably far more effective than Ethiopia. The overall rankings suggested in the table contain few surprises for the informed observer.

Table 1: Ranking of Government Effectiveness ('0' is global average)

Botswana	0.87	Tanzania	-0.51	Ethiopia	-0.89
Mauritius	0.53	Benin	-0.62	Zambia	-0.93
South Africa	0.52	Cameroon	-0.62	Sudan	-1.11
Namibia	0.18	Sao Tome	-0.64	Nigeria	-1.12
Ghana	0.01	Malawi	-0.68	Angola	-1.16
Seychelles	0	Burkina Faso	-0.69	Togo	-1.17
Mauritania	-0.16	Chad	-0.75	Congo	-1.25
Senegal	-0.18	Guinea	-0.78	Guinea-Bissau	-1.35
Cape Verde	-0.2	Niger	-0.79	E. Guinea	-1.37
Lesotho	-0.26	Zimbabwe	-0.8	CAR	-1.43
Madagascar	-0.38	Gambia	-0.81	Burundi	-1.46
Mozambique	-0.41	Rwanda	-0.82	Liberia	-1.51
Uganda	-0.41	Comoros	-0.84	Sierra Leone	-1.54
Eritrea	-0.44	Mali	-0.84	Congo, Dem. Rep.	-1.6
Swaziland	-0.44	Kenya	-0.85	Somalia	-1.97
Gabon	-0.45	Cote d'Ivoire	-0.89		

Source: Derived from World Bank Governance Indicators, 1996-2002. Found at: http://www.worldbank.org/wbi/governance/govdata2002/index.html. Viewed on 26 March 2005.

While a few of the rankings are impressive (Botswana's score places it just below Italy and just above South Korea), the average African performance is obviously low by global standards. Only six sub-Saharan African countries – Botswana, Mauritius, South Africa, Namibia, Ghana and Seychelles – have measures of government effectiveness that are at or above the world average. The rest are below the global average, most significantly worse than the global norm.

Of course, it could be argued that a global comparison is unfair given vastly different income levels, although investors do search worldwide for the best markets to invest. However, the African performance is also unimpressive compared to most developing countries. The top twenty-four countries on the government effectiveness scale are all developed or close to developed countries. If these are removed from the sample (the Bahamas then becomes the top scorer), the global average is -0.25. Even then, only an additional three African countries (Mauritania, Senegal and Cape Verde) are above what essentially becomes the average for developing countries. Most African countries fall below, some well below, the average for developing countries.

Especially notable in the scores presented in Table 1 is that four (Democratic Republic of Congo, Ethiopia, Nigeria and Sudan) large African countries containing fully 41 per cent of the population of sub-Saharan Africa are in the bottom third of the *African* distribution for government effectiveness.[5] In contrast, there are many small countries (by population) that are relatively well-governed although, quite clearly, there are also a number of small countries that have poor levels of government effectiveness. As a result, the average African undoubtedly experiences even poorer governance than the continental averages suggests because a very large share of the total continental population is located in a few countries that have especially poor levels of governance.

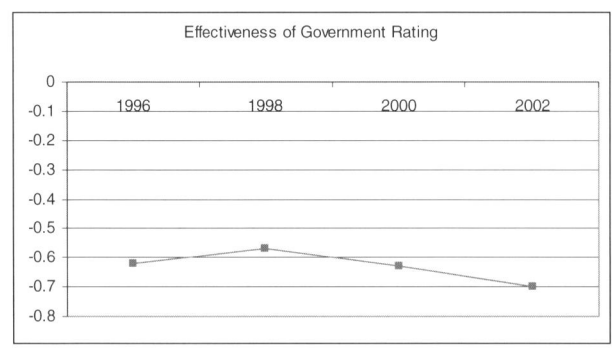

It is especially difficult to discuss trends in African governance over time. Data quality has improved remarkably in the last few years but projecting backward even a relatively few years is still difficult. The World Bank's effectiveness of government

---

[5] The remaining two African countries out of the six most populous are South Africa and Tanzania.

statistic indicates that, relative to the performance of all countries, average African governance performance actually declined relative to the global average in the period 1996-2002. It may have been, of course, that the actual effectiveness of government improved across Africa but simply did so at a slower rate than the rest of the world. The data is weak enough that it is probably only safe to say that government effectiveness across Africa almost certainly did not improve significantly relative to the rest of the world in the period 1996-2002. Such a performance is clearly inadequate given the poverty that afflicts Africa.

Of course, the African average over time does hide substantial changes in individual countries. Table 2 lists those countries that had a change in their effectiveness of government scores of more than 0.5 between 1996 and 2002, a notable change even considering the inherent margins of error in such measures.

Table 2: Most Dramatic Changes in Levels of Government Effectiveness, 1996-2002

Improved Government Effectiveness		Lessoned Government Effectiveness	
Country	Change in Score	Country	Change in Score
Seychelles	.69	Sierra Leone	-1.26
Botswana	.61	Côte d'Ivoire	-0.71
Tanzania	.53	Gambia	-0.68
		Burundi	-0.64
		CAR	-0.62
		Zimbabwe	-0.57
		Guinea-Bissau	-0.53

It may be a coincidence of bad luck that more African countries saw significant declines in government effectiveness than experienced notable gains. However, it is also not hard to conclude that dramatic deteriorations of governance are possible in very short periods of time, especially during periods of conflict. On the other hand, improving levels of government effectiveness relative to the world standard is a slow and difficult process that invariably takes many years.

Part of Africa's governance problem is, as South African President Thabo Mbeki has recently noted, due to perceptions. Not much is known about Africa by investors and others who respond to surveys and the bad news is more familiar than the good. However, even the most basic objective indicators tell basically the same story about African governance. For instance, Table 3 portrays an objective measure of governance: how long does it take to enforce a basic business contract. This is a measure that is immune to the large number of substantive questions that sophisticated measures of governance face and also one that investors, both domestic and foreign, care deeply about.

Table 3: What it takes to Enforce a Contract

Region	Number of Procedures	Days	Region	Number of Procedures	Days
OECD	19	229	Africa	35	434
East Asia	27	316	Middle East	38	437
South Asia	29	349	Latin America	35	462
C. Europe & Central Asia	29	412			

Source: World Bank, 'Doing Business: Benchmarking Business Regulations' database found at: http://rru.worldbank.org/doingbusiness. Viewed 29 March 2005. The Bank notes that the methodology for this indicator was first developed by Simeon Djankov, Rafael La Porta, Florencio Lopez-de-Silanes, and Andrei Shleifer, *Quarterly Journal of Economics*, Vol. 118, pp. 453-517, May 2003.

The African average time for enforcing a contract clearly lags far behind those areas of the world that are growing quickly, although it is no worse than the Middle East or Latin America. Problems in basic governance are hardly limited to Africa but Africa must do far better in order to begin to grow.

Again, when examining the time to enforce a basic business contract, there is substantial variation between African countries. However, the message is essentially the same as portrayed by the government effectiveness variable. Table 4 provides individual country scores while ranking countries on how many days are required to enforce a contract. Again, it is quite clear who are the best and worst scorers on governance in Africa, although the exact rankings of countries between the extremes does vary, hardly a surprise given how difficult it is to assign one numerical value to the constellation of governance issues.

Table 4: What it Takes to Enforce a Contract.

Country	Number of Procedures	Days Required	Country	Number of Procedures	Days Required
Angola	47	1,011	Kenya	25	360
Congo, Dem. Rep.	51	909	Zimbabwe	33	350
Nigeria	23	730	Mali	28	340
CAR	45	660	Niger	33	330
Cameron	58	585	Sierra Leone	58	305
Mozambique	38	580	Lesotho	49	285
Benin	49	570	Madagascar	29	280
Congo, Rep.	47	560	Malawi	16	277
Côte d'Ivoire	25	525	South Africa	26	277
Burundi	51	512	Zambia	16	274
Senegal	36	485	Namibia	31	270
Burkina Faso	41	458	Tanzania	21	242
Ethiopia	30	420	Uganda	15	209
Mauritania	28	410	Ghana	23	200
Rwanda	29	395	Botswana	26	154

Note: Not all African countries were included in the 'Doing Business' database.

Improving African Governance

Even the imperfect measures portrayed above suggest that there is not one African governance problem but (at least) three given the enormous, and increasing, heterogeneity across the continent.

First, there are a group of *relatively well-governed African countries*. These might reasonably be said to include Botswana, Ghana, Mauritius, Namibia, South Africa and possibly a few others at the margin. These countries have already established basic institutions that work relatively well and have begun to register good scores even by global standards. The path to even better performance is relatively straightforward for this group: they must continue to strengthen institutions and adopt best practices as identified by other countries and by international institutions. Improving their performance relative to the rest of the world will not be an easy task but, given how well Botswana is already doing, there is no reason to believe that countries in this group could not have extremely good levels of governance by world standards relatively soon.

That almost all the relatively well-governed African countries are in Southern Africa (although it is certainly not the case that all Southern African countries are well-governed) suggests that the region might have a comparative advantage in governance that could be exploited to attract investors. Indeed, the tragedy of Zimbabwe is particularly poignant because it is the one Southern African country (Angola could reasonably be said not to be in the region) that not only has poor levels of governance but that is actually deteriorating quickly. One of the many ways that Zimbabwe hurts the entire region is that it warns outsiders that there is not yet a complete region-wide consensus on governance in Southern Africa and that reverses are still possible. Thus, a solution to the Zimbabwe problem is very much in the interest of all of Southern Africa.

There is a second group of countries that are *extremely poorly governed*. These might reasonably include Angola, Burundi, CAR, Côte d'Ivoire, DRC, Liberia, Nigeria, Somalia, Sudan, Togo, Zimbabwe and a number of other countries. These countries have yet to establish (or in many cases have destroyed) basic institutions of governance. They are so far from the global norm that it will take many years of work for their actual level of governmental effectiveness to improve. The individual problems of these countries vary – some are in conflict, some are still recovering from conflict, while others have simply been badly governed for many years – and there is obviously no one template that can be applied to all of them. However, the horizon for significant improvements in governance for most of them might reasonably be a decade or more. This is not to say for a moment that dramatic improvements in governance are impossible for this group, just that a reasonable expectation for them achieving significant gains in governance is many years ahead, and they face a completely different set of challenges from the relatively well-governed set of countries.

The large number of African countries that are extremely poorly governed and the significant populations that they contain suggest how hard it will be to improve the African continental average on governance in the near future. Especially if calculations are weighted by population (so that Nigeria counts sixty times as much as Botswana), the struggle to improve African governance is going to be extremely difficult and take a very long time. Such a conclusion has obvious implications for proposals to dramatically increase aid to Africa but also for how the continent is likely to be perceived by the international community in the years ahead.

Perhaps the most interesting group is the third set of countries, those that are *on the cusp of good governance* scores and that cannot reasonably be said to be at either pole of overall performance. These countries are close to performing relatively well, either on the basis of their present scores or due to recent significant upward improvements in their level of performance. While this group is by definition more nebulous, it might reasonably be said to include Kenya (more on the basis of the intentions of the present government than on performance to date), Madagascar, Mozambique, Tanzania, Uganda and some others (including possibly Ethiopia), depending on precisely what measure is used.

This is the most intriguing group of countries because they may be within striking distance of good governance records in the near future. They are also relatively large countries with significant populations. Finally, the concentration of countries in East Africa suggests that, if things were to go well for this group, a second area of Africa could reasonably begin to develop a reputation for good governance. Such a regional development would again be welcome because of its signal to investors and because it might further propel individual countries who wanted to keep up with their neighbours.

There is absolutely no guarantee that the countries on the cusp will actually perform better but they have potential and have solved some basic institutional issues that still bedevil those that are performing poorly. A profound effort at improving governance by the individual governments is obviously an absolute necessity but these countries are also well-positioned to benefit from significant assistance from the international community. Indeed, they might be among the best investments that the international community could make when trying to improve African governance both because they are close to relatively good scores and because the effect across Africa of relatively large countries doing better on governance would be important. If these countries did relatively well, there might also be a positive effect on the perceptions of Africa by the outside world.

These countries could benefit especially from relatively dramatic moves that allow domestic and international audiences to understand the positive developments that are occurring. At the same time, dramatic negative developments in these countries will be especially painful because they could still backtrack. Among the very positive measures that these countries could take would be:

- Routinizaiton of elections. The relatively high scores of Botswana, Namibia and South Africa indicate that rotation of parties in power is hardly a requirement for good governance. However, the coun-

tries with relatively good governance have managed to routinize elections so that voting now occurs without violence and with a minimum number of claims of cheating. The countries on the cusp still have some to significant problems with elections (Madagascar is a dramatic example) and must improve their electoral machinery and level of trust between parties if they are to do better soon.
- Exemplary treatment of corruption. This will further differentiate countries on the cusp from others. All of these countries have significant problems with corruption and are dealing with them in a variety or more-or-less effective ways. A public effort to significantly diminish corruption by punishing powerful actors would be a sign that the governance efforts of these countries is now coming to fruition. The stakes in the struggle over corruption in Kenya are therefore very high but that is simply a more public version of the battle that is occurring in each of these countries.
- Improving property rights through better and easier contract enforcement. This may be a particularly tractable area that will have significant implications for investment. There is significant (by African standards) investor interest in each of these countries but their legal systems cannot be counted upon to help businesses ensure contract enforcement in a timely manner. At the same time, their judicial systems are not generally in as bad a shape as those countries that are performing poorly, so they have potential to do better soon.

There are undoubtedly many other substantive areas where these countries could also improve governance that would signal that they are rising into the top tier of African performers.

Conclusion

The governance story in Africa is complicated both by the difficulty of measuring actual government performance and by the enormous range of performance across the continent. Understanding the very different challenges faced by a variety of countries will be an important step for further analysis and to help individual nations improve. Finally, understanding the particular type of development challenge that each country faces should help predict success in ensuring peace and stability.

The Obstacles to Stability and Security in Africa

Seth Obeng

The story of Africa is one that recounts the distress and subsequent turmoil that tend to emanate from political instability, insecurity, ethnic conflict, poverty, famine hunger and disease. Nowhere on this planet is the level of human deprivation more evident and so overwhelming. Our continent seems to have had more than its fair share of global conflicts, social problems and, often, unmitigated catastrophe.

It has been widely reported that in Africa, HIV/AIDS is in the process of wiping out an entire generation and is already responsible for rendering over 12 million children as orphans.[1] And yet the wealth of the continent is almost immeasurable. Apart from the numerous military interventions on the continent, we have also been plagued by wars which have tended to feed on the numerous destabilizing factors on the continent.

Several reasons account for the lack of stability and security. These include nerve-racking issues emanating from poor governance, inadequate resources for development, rising expectations of a deprived and restive people, as well as, in some cases, unhelpful external influences. All these destabilizing issues can be classified as political and socio-economic factors. In other areas, intriguingly, internally induced factors have co-mingled with externally influenced factors to pose formidable obstacles to stability and security on the continent.

In many cases, political intolerance, ethnic differences and nepotism have also been significant contributory factors. Consequently, there are countless instances of poor governance, a general lack of development or improvement in the lives of the governed, disaffection, protests, confrontation, internal strife and a general state of insecurity which have conjoined to give Africa an unfortunate image.

---

[1] UNAIDS/WHO 2004 Report on the global AIDS epidemic.

Whereas there are clear instances of serious inter-state conflict in Africa, such as evidenced in the Eritrea-Ethiopia conflict or such protracted conflicts as that in Western Sahara, and to a lesser degree the skirmishes between externally backed rebel forces and state governments in West Africa, by and large, our problems have been predominantly intra-state and effectively internally induced. Africa is therefore engaged in what is commonly referred to as 'non-international armed conflict' – that is, conflict in which national armed forces are pitched against other armed groups within a given state.

Stability

Generally, a state of political stability connotes one in which real or imaginary notions of the violent disruption in government administration are absent. This desirable state of mind is achievable when a people consider a government as both legitimate and capable of maintaining the general expectations of the greatest number of citizens. When this state of mind prevails in any state there is no general desire to resort to a violent change of government. Such legitimacy is best initiated through the ascendancy to power of a set of state officials, through institutionalized and accepted processes. These processes must also be associated with transparency and fairness and must be devoid of coercion or other undue forms of suppression and general injustice.

Stability may also be measured by the institutionalized regularity and smoothness of changes of government based on the popular will. It is also a reflection of the quality of governance. Sadly, however, some notable international commentators on the political scene in Africa have often described some elections on the continent as a charade of democracy. Additionally, current views vary significantly on what constitutes political legitimacy. My own thinking is that even though a state of political stability may be achievable in a given political entity, the seeds of future conflict will have been effectively sowed if a generally upheld notion of illegitimacy can at any stage be tagged to a subsequent government.

Security

The vital concept of security has sometimes been referred to as the absence of conflict, or the capacity to sustain a military and economic posture which is sufficiently strong to deter both internal and external forms of aggression. Security in the modern sense therefore means much more to the student of

Strategic Studies. Hence, the significance of the events of 9/11 in the United States has provided an important aspect in current thinking on internal security with which the discipline of Strategic Studies is rightly contending.

Security may be discussed in various terms, namely: national security; regional or sub-regional security; and international or global security. All of these are of relevance to the countries of Africa. However, in our environment we tend to speak not only of physical security or military might, but more importantly, in other terms such as food security, water security, security of the environment, security against the proliferation of arms and ammunition, international terrorism, effects of religious and sectional fanaticism, drug-trafficking, child-trafficking and slavery. Other important strands relate to security against the exportation or dumping of industrial waste, expired pharmaceutical and food products including poultry and meat products to Africa. These are issues which have great relevance to Africa, a deprived continent where the concept of a 'fast buck' poses peculiar threats to morality, unconventional earning opportunities and for our purposes, stability and security.

With the foregoing, certain questions emerge. For instance, how can we feel secure at a time like this when globalization, so popularly termed, ostensibly offers a congenial environment for trade, development and growth but also has seriously negative consequences for our economies? What are the consequent implications for our future as a people? How can we feel secure when we are already at a disadvantage in external trade? How can we feel secure when basic human needs like good health, water and food are not within the reach of a significant size of our populations?

Stability as an issue on the African continent is often seen by some academics as crucial to global security. This view is based upon the perception that if the continent is allowed to wallow in its present abject poverty, hunger and disease, then it would serve as a breeding ground for future violence for both the continent and the rest of the world. Even though there is some credibility in these thoughts, it is nevertheless important to see African development as the basic requirement and objective for the long-suffering but good people of Africa in this context, and not necessarily as a means of promoting some exogenous interests.

Good Governance

I have already referred to governance as an essential ingredient for stability and security. Good governance is a foundation for sound democracy, especially since its implementation demands the application of the rule of law. It also promotes transparency and ensures justice and equity for all citizens, no matter their sex, ethnicity, religion or level of education. In addition, good governance caters for education, health and other social services. It provides for adequate remuneration for work done. It guarantees basic liberties and human rights. It is devoid of coercion. Good governance is therefore what most African states have since independence been struggling to attain. Now, however, the proverbial wind of change is blowing on the continent – hastened, arguably, by the collapse of communism in Eastern Europe.

Capacity for Response

The lack of capacity to respond to looming threats to security has also over the years had a telling effect on how disputes have been managed on the continent. The poor economies of many African countries have consigned some of our military forces into pale shadows of veritable fighting forces. Basic requirements such as transport, arms and radios are unfortunately limited. In most cases mobilization and troop deployment have taken so long that the concept of rapid response and the collation of relevant intelligence have been appalling.

The ECOWAS Monitoring Group (ECOMOG) operations in Liberia in the 1990s, and more recently in 2004, attest to the consequences of a lack of capacity for timely response. Again, our commitment to show a presence in the Darfur region of Sudan was never matched by our practical actions. These two instances point to a real lack of capacity for timely and effective response to difficulties before they assume proportions that require much more resources and effort.

The lack of capacity is gravely worsened by the absence of a reliable and well-co-ordinated and efficient earlywarning mechanism to alert governments or relevant international bodies about looming threats to peace and security. This deficiency is not only prevalent within the sub-regional organizations but more seriously also on a continental basis as an instrument in the hands of the African Union. There is no denying the fact that sometimes the inertia is due to the unwillingness or inability to take obvious and relevant measures necessary to curb further escalation of disputes.

External Influences
One may be forgiven for thinking that whenever there is conflict in any part of the continent, it serves the interests of not only constituencies within the countries in which such conflicts rage, but also external groups including other states or governments. At the height of the Cold War, many military interventions seemed to have been orchestrated by external forces, or at least supported by such external sources. Although there appeared to be a change from about the late 1980s, I believe that traces of the old hypothesis persist. Last year, for example, some foreign nationals with questionable motives were arrested in Zimbabwe, ostensibly preparing to destabilize Equatorial Guinea. The difficulties the West Africa sub-region has experienced within the last fifteen years have also been largely inflamed by the insertion of foreign fighters in the conflicts in Liberia and Sierra Leone.

Even in Côte d'Ivoire unconfirmed reports suggest the presence or influence of foreign military advisers and perhaps fighters. Even more shocking have been the recent revelations that last year, a UN report about an invasion of the Democratic Republic of Congo by Rwanda was full of false claims. Obviously, such claims and reports are intended to destabilize the peace process in a way that serves the interests of some faceless individuals or groups or even governments. These external players seem to exploit prevailing local grievances to engineer conflict or support internal factions that would best serve their interests. Indeed, the end of the Cold War has exposed deep-rooted social and political problems not only in Europe but also in Africa and other parts of the world.

Summary
The following political and socio-economic causal factors should serve as a basis for future discussions on stability and security in Africa. They can generally be grouped into two significant clusters of factors, namely:

a. *Political Factors*
    (1) Poor Leadership
    (2) Bad Governance
    (3) Military Interventions
    (4) External influences, including the proliferation of small arms and foreign fighters

b. *Socio-Economic Factors*
    (1) Mismanagement of resources
    (2) Poor infrastructure, including social services
    (3) Unemployment
    (4) Poverty
    (5) Tribalism and nepotism giving rise to cleavages in society
    (6) Unresolved internal disputes or conflicts, sometimes laced with religious animosities

Many of the aforementioned factors are quite inter-related. Naturally, therefore, the interplay between these largely internal factors and external influences coming from diverse interest groups and international players have had their part in either ameliorating or aggravating the stability and security conditions that prevail on the continent.

Finally, fate has appointed us to be at this venue – Tswalu – at a time like this, when the world expects Africa to come out from a state of near marginalization unto the arena where concerns of the future are discussed to help establish peace and stability in our backyards.

Development as a Strategic Concern: Re-orienting the Response to Faltering States

Kurt Shillinger

For five years, as Robert Mugabe has systematically dismantled the institutions of democracy in Zimbabwe and sent the economy reeling, South Africa, perhaps the only country in the world in a position to leverage Harare, has actively shielded Mugabe from criticism and punitive measures in the United Nations, the Commonwealth and the African Union, and rushed to legitimize three elections in Zimbabwe that were manifestly undermined by state-sponsored violence and orchestrated ballot fraud. In the interim, Zimbabwe has gone from being a member of the Commonwealth and International Monetary Fund to an 'outpost of tyranny' – a distinction the United States bestows currently on only five other countries: Belarus, Cuba, Myanmar, Iran and North Korea. The commercial agriculture sector has been destroyed, the judiciary made subservient to the ruling party and the independent and foreign media muzzled. Inflation stands currently at 127 per cent, down from a peak of 623 per cent; the unemployment rate hovers as high as 80 per cent, according to some estimates; exports are down by two-thirds and the currency is in freefall.[1]

Pretoria has consistently characterized its policy options in Zimbabwe as a stark either/or choice between two extremes: soft diplomacy or hard invasion. This is certainly simplistic, but in an age of global asymmetric threats, it is also dangerous. The case of Mohamed Suleman Vaid shows why.

On 25 April 2001, Vaid, a resident of the South African port of Durban, was arrested along with his wife while attempting to smuggle $130,000 in local currency across the border into Swaziland.[2] The ensuing

---

[1] 'Zimbabwe's economy falls on its knees', *Mail and Guardian*, www.mg.co.za, 26 March 2005. See also Zimbabwe country reports, www.imf.org.
[2] Robert Block, 'In South Africa, Case of Cash Courier Smells of al Qaeda Activity,' *Wall Street Journal*, 10 December 2002, p. 1.

police investigation indicated ties to the terrorist network Al-Qa'ida. Vaid, who denied any connection with such groups, was carrying the funds to a Lebanese businessman in Mozambique who allegedly did have such links. Vaid's arrest was not the result of vigilant customs control. In fact, it was subsequently established that he had made 150 trips to Mozambique in the preceding eighteen months – roughly once every four days. On the day of his arrest, Vaid had stuffed 2.25 kilograms of South African bank notes into his underpants. The resulting effect this had on his gait caught the authorities' attention. Vaid's wife, it was discovered, had more than twice as much cash hidden beneath her traditional veil in a special body suit.

In the wake of 9/11 the street-level assumption is that South Africa is a haven of relative safety, beset by domestic crime but far from the main theatres of modern terrorism and counter-terrorism. The current level of detected suspicious activity could be construed as confirmation of this. As one Western diplomat based in the country put it, South Africa is more likely to be an 'R&R' destination than a target or operational base for terrorists.[3] Pretoria's efforts to strengthen police and intelligence capabilities and its close co-operation with Western counterparts since the 9/11 attacks have been instrumental in making South Africa a more problematic environment for terrorists. But the government's coddling of weak neighbouring regimes such as Zimbabwe and Swaziland, combined with a range of other factors – the region's interconnected physical, communications and banking infrastructure; its porous borders and sea ports; its mineral wealth; its distance from the current epicentre of global terrorism and counter-terrorism; its preponderance of Western targets; its under-resourced and ill-trained national and regional security branches; a rising influx of illegal Pakistani immigrants in South Africa; and the demonstrable susceptibility to radicalization of South Africa's large Muslim population – nonetheless render the region highly vulnerable. Pretoria's failure to intervene more effectively to prevent Zimbabwe's crisis, therefore, has broader ramifications in an interconnected world.

Two urgent questions thus arise: First, what forms of external engagement are required to help weak states help themselves? And second, how should the international community redefine the rules of diplomacy and reorient national and international institutions to respond to the threats posed by weak states in the post-9/11 age?

---

[3] Interview, February 2005.

New Dangers, Old Tools

Prior to the attacks in Washington and New York on 11 September 2001, international development was defined largely in humanitarian terms. Hunger, illiteracy and high child mortality rates were unacceptable social conditions in a civilized world. That remains true, but 9/11 has added a new urgency. Uplifting dysfunctional states is no longer primarily just a matter of morality or, more cynically, economic self-interest. In the age of globalized terrorism, development must be defined fundamentally as a strategic concern. On 19 September 2002 the Bush administration released its National Security Strategy, stating:

> *The events of September 11, 2001 taught us that weak states, like Afghanistan, can pose as great a danger to our national interests as strong states. Poverty does not make poor people into terrorists and murderers. Yet poverty, weak institutions, and corruption can make weak states vulnerable to terrorist networks and drug cartels within their borders.*[4]

In June 2004 the bipartisan US Commission on Weak States and National Security, in its report 'On the Brink: Weak States and US National Security', defined weak states as those where governments are

> *unable to do the things that their own citizens and the international community expect from them: protecting people from internal and external threats, delivering basic health services and education, and providing institutions that respond to the legitimate demands and needs of the population.*[5]

Weak states, the report notes, pose risks to international security in five ways:
- They produce *spill over effects* such as the cross-border flow of refugees, disease, drugs, arms, ideologies and violence.
- They provide relaxed security environments from which *illicit transnational networks* such as terrorist and criminal groups can operate.
- They undermine *regional security*, particularly in cases where the dominant power, such as Nigeria, the Democratic Republic of Congo and Pakistan, is dysfunctional.
- They limit the impact on regional and global *economic progress* by affecting lawful exploitation and flow of critical resources.

---

[4] At www.whitehouse.gov/nsc/nss.html.
[5] See www.cgdev.org/weakstates for the full report.

- They impose *moral burdens* on global powers such as the United States, which risk losing credibility among poor, marginalized or politically excluded population groups for failing to act against corrupt or brutal regimes.

Weak states are most prevalent among the seventy-seven lowest ranked countries on the UN Human Development Index, which measures such factors as life expectancy, literacy rates, access to clean water, child nutrition and percentage of people living below the income poverty line, and notes the correlative relationship between these factors and economic growth and good governance. The most extreme examples are Somalia, Haiti and, prior to the US invasion in late 2001, Afghanistan, where government, economic and civil society structures have almost or completely ceased to function. In the heightened international security environment that now pertains, however, it is arguable – indeed demonstrable – that these cases pose less risk globally than the dozens of states where some level of governance exists, enabling varying levels of economic activity within a context otherwise marked by poor national security and, too often, corruption and political intolerance. Importantly, all of the countries in Africa that currently pose the greatest concern to the US in terms of international terrorism – these include the Sahelian states and, in the Horn, Kenya, Tanzania and Ethiopia – rank in the bottom tier of the most recent UN HDI.[6] None is on target to reach the UN Millennium Development Goals (MDGs) of halving poverty by 2015.

A number of initiatives have been launched since the start of 2005 to address the needs of weak states, including the British Prime Minister Tony Blair's Commission on Africa and plans by the UN and the World Bank to realize the MDGs. These approaches embrace measures such as doubling aid, cutting debt and dismantling barriers to trade to enable poor states, particularly those in Africa, to escape what Columbia University economist Jeffrey Sachs calls the 'poverty trap'. This, Sachs argues, requires a 'big push' in seven areas: raising rural productivity; tackling the disease burden; making primary education universal and expanding secondary education; financing urban development; mobilizing science and technology; gender equality; and regional integration.

But there is no reason to expect that massive infusions of cash will solve these problems. Aid levels to sub-Saharan Africa in the mid-1990s

---

[6] For the full report, see www.undp.org.

reached as high as 9.3 per cent of the recipient states' gross national product. By comparison, aid to post-war Europe under the Marshall Plan never exceeded 2.5 per cent of GNP. Indeed, despite receiving more than $500 billion in foreign aid over the past five-plus decades, most African states are poorer today per capita than they were in 1970. Indeed, a critical lesson from the post-colonial Asian experience – and, indeed, post-apartheid South Africa – is that countries make economic progress when they possess, above all, the political will to do so. Vietnam, for example, according the World Bank, reduced poverty from 51 per cent in 1990 to 14 per cent in 2002.

The critical challenge, therefore, in a world where security is increasingly dependent upon solving the problem of state dysfunction, is to impose the conditions requisite for successful and sustained development where the local political impetus is deficient. Doing so requires re-imagining the way nations talk to each other across the North-South divide and creating new national and international institutions designed to respond to current global imperatives rather than reforming those that were established to serve the security needs of an age that has past.

Toward A New Global Dialogue

Halving poverty, reversing the spread of HIV/AIDS, cutting maternal and child mortality rates and providing universal primary education are all noble pursuits. Eliminating the barriers to equitable trade between industrialized and developing nations is imperative. Creating a more representative UN Security Council is requisite. But the current international dialogue, marked by a rising clamour among developing nations for global rebalance, remains predicated on a fundamental *quid pro quo* relationship between the haves and have-nots. Tying aid to good governance is the clearest example of this, but the abiding paradigm of conditionality increasingly runs both ways. More importantly, while the concentration of global wealth in a minority of nations is now widely recognized as unsustainable, the measures so far proposed to correct this imbalance have brought little effect. The International Criminal Court, for example, may allow for tyrants to be tried if they are caught, but it is powerless to prevent state collapse.

In an age of urgent and inter-connected security concerns, what, then, is needed?

The British diplomat Robert Cooper argues the case for what he calls 'the voluntary imperialism of the global economy' and 'the imperialism of neighbours'.[7] The former involves a states submitting to the terms and conditions of international financial institutions such as the International Monetary Fund. But such engagement, in the form of economic structural adjustment programmes, has produced little lasting benefit, particularly in Africa. The latter, Cooper argues, involves foreign military and economic intervention through mechanisms such as UN protectorates and favoured terms of trade. These, too, have had only limited success.

Other approaches include, as former Sudanese Prime Minister Imaan Sadiq Al-Mahdi advocates, creating a UN economic security council.[8] Edward Luttwak has argued the potential long-term stabilizing effect of allowing war to run its course.[9] Greg Mills, meanwhile, points out the limitations of 'international trusteeship' – such as the administrative role taken on by the UN in Sierra Leone.[10] And the South African experience in Zimbabwe underscores the pitfalls of placing too much reliance on a single state to prevent state collapse in another, particularly where domestic and/or historic imperatives are apparent.

Addressing state weakness arguably requires a multi-layered approach involving both a range of elements that have been utilized individually as well as the creation of new structures based on new rules of partnership and engagement. Current national and international institutions are hobbled by their own deeply entrenched bureaucratic cultures. International constellations such as the G8 and the EU, meanwhile, remain Northern-dominated constructs despite their increasing interaction with key Southern counterparts.

A new North-South grouping of states is needed, drawing together the wealthiest and most influential players from both hemispheres. The purpose of this body, which for argument sake I will call the Global

---

[7] Robert Cooper, 'The Post-Modern State,' in *Reordering the World: The Long-Term Implications of September 11*, The Foreign Policy Centre, London, 2002.

[8] Described in a talk given at the South African Institute of International Affairs on 20 April 2005.

[9] Edward Luttwak, 'Give war a chance', *Foreign Affairs* (Vol. 78, No. 4, July/August 1999).

[10] Greg Mills, *The Security Intersection: The paradox of power in an age of terror* (Johannesburg: Wits University Press, 2005), p. 248.

Council of States, would be to prevent conflict and state collapse, in the first instance, and engage in long-term state-building, in the second. How these would be accomplished must be predicated both on establishing a new global consensus on threats embracing the North's preoccupation with terrorism and drug-trafficking with the South's abiding concerns over poverty, disease, fractured civil warfare and ethnic-based genocide, and on new rules of conduct among member states. Intervention in states at risk, such as Zimbabwe, would no longer be left to a single actor, but rather a number of Council member states from both sides of the North-South divide.

Engagement, meanwhile, would be based on a concept introduced at the 3rd Tswalu Dialogue in 2004, and already practiced by Australia in the South Pacific region: embedded support.[11] In its expanded form, this would involve deploying not just security forces from the Council member states, but also businessmen, judges, bankers, academics, engineers, scientists, political and financial advisers, health practitioners and so on. Aid would be targeted toward infrastructure and the development of an entrepreneurial sector. Council states would also undertake to educate the 'client state's' best students in their own universities in a programme where full funding is predicated on the student's agreement to return home upon graduation to a foreign-subsidized job in the sector for which they were trained.

The attacks of 11 September 2001 launched the world into an age that must be defined by long-term strategic developmental engagement between rich and poor nations. This lesson, even if acknowledged, has not yet been realized in policy. The US-led wars in Afghanistan and Iraq continue to reflect a predisposition toward limited intervention based on only the most immediate elements of state-building: the holding of elections and training of local security forces. This same approach characterizes South Africa's diplomatic interventions in such countries as Ivory Coast, the Democratic Republic of Congo and Burundi. A more coherent and sustained project is required. Cost can no longer be held as a prohibitive factor. As the current push toward vastly expanded aid programmes shows, it has already been recognized that investment in strengthening weak states

---

[11] Ian Wilcock, 'Peacekeeping and Peace-Building in the Pacific – Lessons and Trends for International Best Practice,' in Richard Cobbold and Greg Mills, eds, 'Global Challenges and Africa: Report of the 2004 Tswalu Dialogue,' *Whitehall Paper 62*, Royal United Services Institute, London, 2004, p. 105.

is the cheaper alternative to collapse. It is also, in the current context, a security imperative.

Health, Wealth, Terrorism and Energy: A Portent of Western Security Dilemmas in Africa

Greg Mills

Five sets of statistics illustrate the African security dilemma, especially as it pertains to external – especially Western – interests.

1. Energy

Africa is a new, increasingly important energy frontier.

Currently, the US imports two-thirds of its oil needs, and 15 per cent of this comes from Africa. This figure could increase to 25 per cent by 2015. The second-largest energy importer behind the US, China currently imports six million barrels of oil a day. The figure is expected to double in the next fifteen years. With only half of its energy needs now supplied by domestic sources, China is aggressively pursuing fresh oil interests in Africa, notably in the Sudan (which makes up one-tenth of all Chinese oil imports[1]) but also more recently in Angola, where China agreed to a US$2 billion credit line in 2004. Today, the China National Petroleum Corporation (CNPC) is the largest investor in Sudan. CNPC's Heglig and Unity fields in Sudan now produce 350,000 barrels per day. CNPC owns most of a field in southern Darfur, which began trial production in 2004, and 41 per cent of a field in the Melut Basin, which is expected to produce as much as 300,000 barrels per day by the end of 2006. Another Chinese firm, Sinopec Corporation, is erecting a pipeline from that complex to Port Sudan on the Red Sea, where China's Petroleum Engineering Construction Group is constructing a tanker terminal.[2]

In Southern Africa, Angola is at the centre of the oil boom, with its output increasing from 722,000 barrels a day in 2001 to 930,000 in 2003. By 2020, it is expected to reach 3.3 million barrels a day. Nigeria's output is pre-

---

[1] At http://www.energybulletin.net/3753.html.
[2] At http://www.energybulletin.net/3753.html.

dicted to double to 4.4 million barrels a day by 2020. And today's minor oil producers – such as Equatorial Guinea, Chad and Sudan – could more than treble their output given this demand. Today's dozen African producers could in the next few years include five more, including outside of western Africa: Tanzania, Kenya, Uganda, Mozambique and Madagascar.

If Goldman Sachs are to be believed, oil at over US$100 per barrel will thus offer something of a bonanza for certain African governments, but not necessarily for their citizenry, at least if the past (and current) record of the distribution of African oil revenues is anything to go by. Despite, for example, US$350 billion in net oil revenues in thirty-five years, the number of Nigerians living under the international poverty datum line of one dollar per day has risen from 19 million in 1970 (out of a population of 70 million) to 90 million (from a population of 120+ million) in 2000, and where its income inequality is today worse than neighbouring Ghana. On welfare indicators (education, life expectancy, literacy, infant mortality), Africa's oil producers have performed no better than other African countries. They also 'cluster near the bottom' of Transparency International's Corruption Perceptions Index, where oil revenues 'can dangerously distort institutions and politicians' incentives and behaviour'.[3] The latter would include President Bongo's Transgabonais railway in Gabon, the Ajaokuta steel project in Nigeria, which used up several billion dollars but did not produce a single slab in twenty-five years, and the general inflationary impact on the bureaucracies of African petro-states, which seldom indicated their efficiency. The patronage-clientalistic networks on which some African governments have relied have also not encouraged saving but instead an insatiable appetite for spending among key constituencies – not least as it is politically difficult 'to justify saving for the poor than it is for the rich'.[4]

Few jobs have been directly created in this sector, while their economies have suffered from relative decline in the non-oil sector, partly due to the rise in real exchange rates from oil incomes (an effect known as the 'Dutch disease'), a tendency exacerbated by oil price (and thus revenue) volatility and huge borrowings based on over-optimistic forecasting. The 'boom and bust' cycle has predictably affected the poorest hardest and widened income inequalities in the oil producers – even though the differ-

---

[3] See Nicholas Shaxson, 'New approaches to volatility: dealing with the 'resource curse' in sub-Saharan Africa', *International Affairs* (Vol. 81, No. 2, 2005), pp. 311-12.
[4] *Ibid*, p. 319.

ence between first-time 'production' and 'price' windfalls should be recognized.

Yet the scale and future prospects of the oil sector in Africa means, in the words of one executive,[5] 'that there is nothing in Africa that even comes close in terms of investor interest. There is a frenzy of appetite involving American, European and now Chinese and Indian players'. New, large-scale discoveries 'could change Africa irrevocably given the numbers involved'.

But this knowledge has to be tempered against African governance and historical realities and the preferred operating strategy of many foreign oil interests in the continent. As the same oil executive argues, such a boom is 'both good and bad news for Africa: Good news in the sense of the potential for tremendous income. Bad news,' he notes, 'in that the takings and stakes could be much higher now for crooks'. To make sure that this sector makes a positive difference, attention should be focused both on conditions of external and internal governance, especially given that the mainly offshore sector does not benefit the population directly through large-scale employment or services, but only indirectly through taxation.

In summary, the quest for 'energy security' in Africa is a reality in a post-9/11, post-Saddam world; though it is unclear – and some would argue unlikely – whether this boom will enhance the security of Africans unless there is a significant improvement in governance.

2. Wealth

Currently an estimated 40 per cent of (sub-Saharan) Africans, or 250 million people, live below the international poverty datum line of US$1 per day.

This extraordinary statistic reflects Africa's declining relative position in international trade and investment. Africa's share of trade with the West has declined significantly, from 7 per cent of global GDP in 1950 to 2 per cent today. This is partly due to failings and weaknesses in African economies, but is also due to the decline in global commodity prices and the concomitant reliance of Africa on this narrow range of products. The high cost of doing business in Africa has deterred foreign and local investment. The global share of African states of global capital fell during the 1990s from 6 per cent in 1950 to 1 per cent today. In the 1980s, Africa

---

[5] Telephonic discussion, Johannesburg, 17 April 2005.

received around 30 per cent of global foreign direct investment in developing countries; today it is around just 7 per cent.

Yet Africa's loss of an estimated US$275+ billion (including interest) in domestic capital flight since independence (nearly one-and-a-half times the continent's debt stock) suggest that the continent is not without its riches even if most of its people are poor – and that any plan for African recovery and stability has to involve, again, more than just extra flows of money.

3. Health

Africa's health environment remains dangerous and vulnerable. Malaria cases in Africa account for around 90 per cent of the global total. There are an estimated 300-500 million cases each year, causing 1.5 to 2.7 million deaths. More than 90 per cent of the deaths are in children under five years of age in Africa. Malaria ranks third among major infectious disease threats in Africa after pneumococcal acute respiratory infections (3.5 per cent) and tuberculosis (TB) (2.8 per cent).[6]

Also in the health sector, the sub-Saharan Africa region currently has the highest rate, too, of HIV infection worldwide. An estimated 24.5 million (71 per cent) of the world's 34.3 million AIDS cases are in the sub-continent. Nearly 19 million have died from AIDS, 3.8 million of them children under the age of fifteen. Among the other statistics:[7]

- 5.4 million new AIDS infections in 1999, 4 million of them in Africa.
- 2.8 million dead of AIDS in 1999, 85 per cent of them in Africa.
- 13.2 million children orphaned by AIDS, 12.1 million of them in sub-Saharan Africa.
- Reduced life expectancy in sub-Saharan Africa from 59 years to 45 between 2005 and 2010, and in Zimbabwe from 61 to 33.
- Around 500,000 babies infected annually by their mothers, most of them in sub-Saharan Africa.

The economic and security costs of this epidemic are difficult to discern, though the welfare implications – of the impact on families, children and support structures – are manifest.

The continent's inability to deal with the HIV/AIDS epidemic

---

[6] At http://www.ifrc.org/WHAT/health/archi/fact/fmalar.htm.
[7] At http://www.cnn.com/SPECIALS/2000/aids/stories/overview/

reflects in part weak systems of governance and chronically low levels of resistance and nutrition. Similarly diabolical statistics can be extracted for largely preventable water-borne diseases in Africa.

4. Terrorism and Globalization

There is an awareness post-9/11 that the persistence of state atrophy in Africa does not serve Western security interests, offering potentially a source of recruits and operating base for terrorists, a fear no doubt heightened by the relative absence of state presence and high (and some say increasing) percentage of Africans who are Muslim and Islamist. The absence of 'friendly' partners has been exacerbated by the inability of local African police and military institutions to deal with insecurities, and by the relative failure of Western assistance efforts to strengthen capacity in these areas.

But the identification of state weakness is far easier than creating capacity, though the sorts and sequencing of reforms necessary in Africa demand a strong state with a legal-rational bureaucratic basis – but where, instead, 'the Western model of a state is (unsurprisingly) largely absent [and] where, rather, the exercise of personalized exchange, clientelism and corruption is internalized and constitutes "essential operating codes for politics" in a wide variety of spaces'.[8]

5. Failed External Assistance

Finally, the attempts led by Western states to deal with state volatility and insecurity in Africa have produced few encouraging results.

The record of aid expenditure in Africa is dismal with, at best, isolated successes. Forty years of overseas aid to Africa – accumulating to a figure of around US$800 billion – has left the continent no richer today than it was thirty years ago. Certainly, a lot of this assistance was misplaced and squandered. During the Cold War years bilateral external engagement with Africa was driven principally by a combination of superpower strategic self-interest, including the need to secure precious commodities and maintain ideological influence, and colonial legacy. Where human rights

---

[8] Michael Bratton and Nic van de Walle, *Democratic experiments in Africa: regime transitions in comparative perspective* (Cambridge: Cambridge University Press, 1997), p.63 cited in Taylor, *op cit*, p.306.

concerns featured, this motivation was generally limited to concern over transferring white minority to black majority rule, even though by the end of the 1980s such concerns increasingly featured in support for the most egregious of black African leadership, including Mobutu in Zaire, Siad Barre in Somalia and Samuel Doe's Liberia.

Also, as the figure of investment share indicates, liberalization strategies have been equally unsuccessful in spurring greater interest in and higher amounts of capital flows to Africa. This is partly a problem of agency: that the external agencies of the World Bank and the international financial community have been the primary motivator of structural adjustment inevitably undermined, to an extent, the credibility of these programmes, no matter how sensible their logic. For a continent subjected to the worst of colonial excesses, a cry of 'neo-imperialism' has proven an effective way to discount conditionalities. Moreover, the African condition illustrates that macro-liberalization policies in the absence of specific micro-reforms and policy to directly seek out investment is an insufficient, if necessary, economic policy condition.

How might these five different security 'threads' – energy, health, wealth, terrorism and globalization, and external assistance – play themselves out? Let me offer two scenarios: predictably, perhaps, a 'bad' and a 'better' one each.

A 'Bad' Scenario

This scenario is, sadly and rather predictably, not that difficult to write since it simply extends the downward trajectory of African states over the past forty years. Of course, this is not fair on all African states or leaders. There are the oft-cited exceptions – including Botswana, Ghana post-1985, Mozambique, Mauritius and South Africa post-1994. But these are a distinct minority, and in Mozambique's case, it has still a way to go to reach pre-independence standards of living. Nor is such an assessment fair on African peoples, most of whom have toiled long and hard for very little reward over two generations.

Nonetheless, this future 'bad' scenario is different from simple decay – today mainly due to the trifecta of health, wealth through oil and the globalization-terrorism phenomenon.

In this scenario, the voracious US and China economies not only compete for access to Africa's lucrative oil reserves, but display scant regard for governance niceties in doing so. European competitors do not offer an attractive rival vision. African governments, while displaying increasingly differentiated governance standards on paper, prefer to close ranks around the worst excesses of African leadership, thus undermining universal attempts at African reform – such as posited through Nepad.

Thus, rather than states increasingly being positively affected by revitalized state structures, the competition for oil resources drives the standards of governance lower. Foreign actors close ranks around incumbent militaries and other centres of power in the search for investment security but also to ensure greater domestic capacity to meet internal threats and to fight terrorism, but in so doing tighten the grip of ruling parties and elites in power. Government may strengthen in this scenario, but does not necessarily democratize or extend benefits to its citizenry.

In this scenario, less operating space is given to foreign and local NGOs attempting to open up the governance space, with the state employing the chestnuts of 'security needs' and 'nationalism' to marginalize their operations.

While aid flows might, in this scenario, actually increase, the goals are not necessarily development-directed, but rather aimed at security, while there remains the related ongoing disjuncture between commitment and spending, and in terms of the (lack of) co-ordination between spenders. While the link between poverty and conflict is recognized – in the words of UK Secretary of State for International Development Hilary Benn, 'Poverty is both a cause and an effect of human insecurity in developing countries'[9] – this requires the fostering of sound governance beyond the military. Moreover, in this scenario the new, post-9/11, Afghanistan and Iraq security imperatives fritter away spending on African development. This also raises questions about the sustainability of projected increases.

Well-meaning but misplaced attempts to roll-out anti-retroviral HIV treatment in Africa could, in conditions of minimal government, actually worsen the longer-term effects of the disease, encouraging the emergence of drug-resistant strains.

At best, this scenario offers 'islands of prosperity and security'; indeed, the outcome being thus little improved from what we have today.

A 'Better' Scenario

It is clear that, in spite of what Mugabe says, Africa does not face military threats from outside the continent. Instead, the security threats faced by

---

[9] Speech at the Centre for Global Development, Washington DC, 23 June 2004.

African states are by and large internal and political rather than economic in nature.

Where external grievances exist (i.e., from neighbouring countries or external state and non-state sources), these are often a product of the failure of governments to extend their authority and governance to their legal geographic extremities. This reflects a core insecurity facing Africa today – a combination of weak and unresponsive government, limited resources and political systems that centre on favour and hierarchy, rather than on liberal free-market competition and bottom-up 'people's power'.

Overall, there are three major external factors that will likely dictate external terms of engagement with Africa, and there are also a number that are Africa initiated/driven/dependent. Some of these will shape the nature of African conflict in the future:

- The threat Africa poses in terms of migration, terrorism and social instability, including the 'ripeness' for Islamic fundamentalism within Africa.
- The intensification of a global struggle for scarce resources, especially oil but also including other minerals, such as timber and gems. This likely intensification is related to the emergence of the People's Republic of China's 'mega-economy', but is also due to the anticipated economic and industrial development of those East European countries that are now members of the European Union, who will likely increase their productive capacity fairly dramatically and thus their need for resources.
- The related ebb and flow of ideological and political weight globally, between Washington, Brussels, Beijing and multilateral agencies. Will Africa, in this regard, take the option that offers tougher strings?

But there are positive signs, offering a more positive, 'better' scenario.

Nepad recognizes, however subtly, that the economic challenge in Africa is inherently political. This explains the focus on peer review as a core 'deliverable' for this programme, aimed at improving the standards of continental governance on a country-by-country basis.

Politics have, indeed, been the biggest impediment to better African economic performance over the last four decades, in the form of bad leadership, and weak structures and institutions of governance – all of which were both a reflection of and compounded by the colonial inheritance. Africa's leadership has until now been reluctant to take a firm stance against fellow leadership – this reflecting, at least, the personal and polity trauma of colonialism, the failure of post-colonial regimes and consequent collapse of expectations, and the damage done from Africa being a proxy playground for Soviet Marxism and its ideological counterpart, US-led anti-communism. But there are positive signs: the ending of the crisis in Togo and the engagement over Darfur and Ivory Coast are moot cases in point, as is the creation of an effective – at least on paper – set of African Union institutions, notably including the Peace and Security Council (PSC) as a standing decision-making organ for the prevention, management and resolution of conflicts.

Today, the key African security/stability/prosperity challenge is two-fold: One, to offer better conditions of governance for populations and investors alike, free from political favours and violent threats. Two, to offer related improvements in capacity. Africa has no shortage of economic opportunities. It is that they have gone largely unrecognized and the potential unrealized because of levels of uncertainty, perceived or otherwise.

Let me in conclusion highlight five considerations necessitating a re-jigging of international action in the short term:

- First, Africa's oil boom alone will require a fresh political, military, intelligence and strategic focus on the continent. This dimension and the corresponding need for improved systems of governance is both complicated and has made imperative the fear of terrorist activities originating in Africa.
- Second, related is the need to get investors onside in the oil sector, including particularly those from China and the United States. The important challenge here is: Will companies from both countries – as different as their political systems and traditions are – agree to increased scrutiny and sanction on their activities, and will their African partners prefer those that do offer more transparency? And there are wider strategic, security questions: For example, Sudan is China's largest overseas oil supplier and project, and the PRC is reportedly Sudan's largest supplier of arms, including supplying tanks, fighters, helicopters and small arms for use in the two-decade-old North-South civil war that has killed an estimated two million people and displaced twice this number.[10]

---

[10] At http://www.energybulletin.net/3753.html.

- Third, there is a need for a new aid regime in which there is a degree of balance, consistency and coherence between multilateral and bilateral efforts, with a little less promise and a little more delivery. Aid regimes need to move beyond grand frameworks and grandstanding to setting realistic priorities – to mix my metaphors, to identify and pick off the 'low hanging fruit' to get the development ball rolling. Big terms – 'outsourcing', 'regional integration', 'capacity-building', 'infrastructure', etc. – have to take into account the degree of inter- and intra-governmental co-operation and co-ordination required to see them to fruition, and the degree of specialist knowledge and undertaking necessary. There is also a need for 'certainty' in aid – for example, the knowledge that new flows (especially those to HIV/AIDS) will be sustained in the long term.
- Fourth, the external focus on security capacity-building has to percolate down to security at the most local of levels – to police rather than military forces, especially given that the primary threats to Africans are internal and to their livelihood, and likely to come from the state than from each other.
- Fifth, security assistance strategies towards African states have to be mindful of the broader relationship between poverty, health and security, and have to incorporate elements of each. Military assistance has to include elements of development; just as an overarching development strategy has to incorporate aspects of security assistance, both straddling a mixture of security and development objectives.

Finally, a more positive African future hinges on better governance. Such an improvement is a function of better skills and more capacity, requiring inevitably more money and a transfer of skills and technology. But it is also a function of political will, a quality that African leadership has never had in short supply when mobilizing and working the system for its own ends, but seldom in delivering for the common good. This is why aid alone will not solve Africa's problems, and may only serve to foster an 'illusion of compliance and co-operation'.[11] Securing Western interests in Africa thus lies in strengthening accountability and transparency – in so doing, reinforcing the link between the government and citizenry.

---

[11] Ian Taylor, 'Advice is judged by results, not by intentions: why Gordon Brown is wrong about Africa', *International Affairs* (Vol. 81, No. 2, 2005), p. 303.

Appendix

THE FOURTH TSWALU DIALOGUE

Trade, Development and Security:
All Sides of the Same Coin?

Thursday 28 April 2005–Sunday 1 May 2005

Participants
Adam Roberts (Mr), The Economist, UK
Andrew Stewart (Major-General), British Army, UK
Andrea Ostheimer (Ms), Konrad Adenauer Stiftung, Germany
Ashraf Gamal El Din (Dr), Ministry of Investment, Egypt
Barry Desker (Professor), Institute for Defence and Strategic Studies, Singapore
Carlton Fulford (General), ACSS, US
Christopher Clapham (Professor), Cambridge University, UK
Christopher Coker (Professor), London School of Economics, UK
Ebrahim Ebrahim (Mr), Senior Economic and Political Adviser, Deputy Presidency, SA
Fred Phaswana (Mr), National Chairman, SAIIA; Chair: Transnet, SA
Gary Hawes (Dr), Ford Foundation, SA
Greg Mills (Dr), The Brenthurst Foundation, SA
Gui-xuan Liang, (Mr), Minister Counsellor, Embassy of China, SA
Henri Ranaieoson (Mr), Chief of Staff: Presidency, Madagascar
Holger Dix (Mr), Konrad Adenauer Stiftung, Germany
Iqbal Jhazbay (Professor), UNISA, SA
Isaac Nkama (Mr), Boeing, SA
Jendayi Fraser (HE Dr), US Ambassador to SA
Jeffrey Herbst (Professor), Princeton University, US

Appendix

John Battersby (Mr), SA International Marketing Council, UK
Jonathan Oppenheimer (Mr), De Beers, SA
Kurt Shillinger (Mr), SAIIA: Head, Security and Terrorism Project, SA
Lyal White (Mr), SAIIA: Asia and Latin America Researcher, SA
Lynda Chalker (Baroness), Africa Matters Limited, UK
Michael Power (Dr), Investec, SA
Michael Spicer (Mr), Director: SA Foundation, SA
Mills Soko (Dr), Hluma Research and Business Services; SAIIA Research Associate, SA
Monde Muyangwa (Dr), ACSS, US
Mondli Makhanya (Mr), Editor: Sunday Times, SA
Moses Banda (Dr), Economic Adviser to the President, Zambia
Nic Dawes (Mr), Mail and Guardian, SA
Paraschand Hurry (Mr), COMESA, Zambia
Patrick Smith (Mr), Editor: Africa Confidential, UK
Peregrino Isidro Wanbu Chindondo 'Kasitu' Phoneno (Maj.-Gen), Angolan Defence College, Angola
Peter Draper (Mr), SAIIA: Head, Trade Project, SA
Peter Fabricius (Mr), Foreign Editor: Independent Newspaper Group, SA
Razeen Sally (Dr), Head: London School of Economics Trade Policy Unit, UK
Richard Dowden (Dr), Director, Royal African Society, UK
Richard Gibb (Professor), Plymouth University, UK
Ross Herbert (Mr), Head: SAIIA NEPAD Project, SA
Seth Obeng (Lt.-General), Army Chief of Staff, Ghana
Shannon Field (Ms), Presidential Support Unit, SA
Smuts Ngonyama (Mr), Office of the ANC Presidency, SA
Terence McNamee (Dr), RUSI, UK
Warren Searell (HE Mr), NZ High Commissioner to South Africa, NZ

PROGRAMME

Thursday 28 April 2005
Arrival; settling in
17h30-18h30 Drinks
19h00-19h15 Introduction, Greg Mills; Welcome, Jonathan Oppenheimer
<u>Evening Talk:</u> Jendayi Frazer, 'Ensuring African Security and Development: A US Perspective'

Friday 29 April 2005 Motse
07h00-onwards Breakfast
09h00 *Session One: The Global Environment* (Chair: Carlton Fulford)
Christopher Coker
John Battersby
Andrew Stewart
Shannon Field

Questions:
1. Will there be a new international trade regime that is more favourable to African countries? Will the specific problems of agricultural subsidies be addressed?
2. What resources will the international community provide to promote peace in Africa?
    - Will the international community now depend on African leaders – as in Côte d'Ivoire – to negotiate compromises while maintaining a detached attitude?
    - Has the African demand for peacekeepers exhausted the supply?
3. How will international efforts to fight terrorism affect African countries? Does the war on terror provide specific opportunities for African countries?

10h45 Tea

11h00 *Session Two: 'Goods' and 'Bads': Obstacles for African Stability and Security* (Chair: Lynda Chalker)
Jeffrey Herbst
Ashraf Gamal El-Din
Seth Obeng
Michael Spicer

Appendix

Questions:
1. Does Africa have the potential to improve governance to take advantage of more international trade and aid concessions? Which African countries/regions have the greatest hopes of dramatic forward progress?
2. Will the tempo of conflict in Africa continue to decline or are some countries at risk of new or renewed violence?
3. There are some African countries that have such poor environmental circumstances or that are so ravaged by conflict that development in the near term is not a real possibility. What can the international community do to improve their prospects?

13h30 Lunch – Group Photo

14h30 *Session Three: Trade Obstacles and Prospects for Growth* (Chair: Mondli Makhanya)
Razeen Sally
Paraschand Hurry
Barry Desker

Questions:
1. What is the likely mix of foreign investment, aid and domestic savings that African countries will have to depend upon to promote growth?
2. What do African countries have to do to actually take advantage of decreases in agricultural subsidies?
3. Will growth patterns across the continent continue to diverge? What is the impact of an increasingly heterogeneous Africa for regional organizations?
4. Will African countries be able to develop indigenous economic plans that they can explain to their publics?
5. What are the prospects for poverty reduction in the near future?

20h00 After Dinner Talk: Michael Power: 'The Impact of China's Rise on Geo-Economics'

Saturday 30 April Motse
07h00-onwards Breakfast

Break-away into two groups: Session to run from 08h30-11h15; 11h15-13h00

Group One – Trade: Chaired by Barry Desker:
Topics: Promoting African Trade (Mills Soko); The Impact of China on African Trade (Gui-xuan Liang); The Future for Regional Integration in Africa (Richard Gibb). (Short presentations followed by discussion).

Group Two – Stability and Security: Chaired by Smuts Ngonyama:
Topics: Promoting African Security and Stability (Monde Muyangwa); Terrorism, Nation-Building and Weak States (Kurt Shillinger); Health, Wealth, Environment and Energy Security (Greg Mills). (Short presentations followed by discussion).

13h30 Lunch
14h00 Keynote Lunchtime Talk: Richard Dowden, 'What the external community can do for Africa: Assessing the Report of the Africa Commission'. (Chair: Lynda Chalker)

Afternoon Free/Game Drives/ Walk or Drive to Dune for Supper
20h30 Talk on Stars by Tswalu Staff
Jazz

Sunday 1 May 2005, Lekhaba
07h00-onwards Breakfast
08h15 Depart for Lekhaba (Chair: Fred Phaswana)
09h30 Report-back by Three Rapporteurs from Days One and Two
10h00 Presentations by Peter Draper ('Challenges and Prospects for Partnership and Trade'); Ebrahim Ebrahim ('Prospects for Partnership for Security')
11h00 Concluding Discussions 11h30 Brunch at Waterhole; 13h00/14h00 Depart

Biographies

JOHN BATTERSBY
John Battersby is UK Country Manager of the International Marketing Council of South Africa. He was appointed in January 2004 following a career spanning more than three decades in South African and international journalism. He was formerly editor of the *Sunday Independent* (1996-2001), Political Editor of the *Independent Group* (2001-2003) and southern Africa correspondent for the *New York Times* (1987-89) and the *Christian Science Monitor* (1989-1994) and its Middle East correspondent (1994-96).

CHRISTOPHER COKER
Professor Christopher Coker is Professor of International Relations at the London School of Economics and Political Science. He is author of numerous books on defence and international affairs, including *Twilight of the West, Waging War Without Warriors* (short-listed for the 2003 Duke of Westminster's Medal for Military Literature) and most recently, *The Future of War*.

BARRY DESKER
Ambassador Barry Desker is the Director of the Institute of Defence and Strategic Studies, Nanyang Technological University. He was the Chief Executive Officer of the Singapore Trade Development Board from 1994 to 2000, after serving in the foreign service since 1970. He was Singapore's Ambassador to Indonesia from 1986 to 1993, Director of the Policy, Planning and Analysis Division of the Ministry of Foreign Affairs, 1984-86 and Deputy Permanent Representative to the United Nations, New York, 1982-84. He was educated at the University of Singapore, University of London and Cornell University.

RICHARD DOWDEN
Richard Dowden is Director of the Royal African Society. He first went to Africa and a volunteer teacher in 1971, spending nearly two years in Uganda that coincided with the first years of Idi Amin's rule. He was forced to leave at the end of 1972 and returned in 1983. In the interim he had become a journalist and for the next twenty years, travelled to Africa

continuously and has now visited and written about nearly every country on the continent. He worked for *The Times* until 1986, when he became Africa Editor of the *Independent*. In 1995 he became Africa Editor at *The Economist*. He has also made three television documentaries for the BBC and Channel 4, on Africa.

SHANNON FIELD
Shannon Field is a member of the Presidential Support Unit, and specializes in conflicts on the African continent and in the Middle East. She has worked for the United Nations in the area of peace and security at the UN Staff College, and as the Senior Advisor to the Canadian Secretary of State for Africa. She has been engaged in conflict resolution and peace-building as the Programmes Co-ordinator at ACCORD in Durban, and served as the Deputy Director of the Johannesburg based Institute for Global Dialogue.

JENDAYI FRAZER
Dr Jendayi Frazer is United States Assistant Secretary of State for African Affairs. She served as Special Assistant to the President and Senior Director for African Affairs at the National Security Council from 2001 until her swearing-in as US Ambassador to South Africa in 2004. She came to the NSC from Harvard University, where she was serving as an Assistant Professor of Public Policy at the Kennedy School of Government.

RICHARD GIBB
Dr Richard Gibb is a Reader in Human Geography at the University of Plymouth, United Kingdom. His research interests focus on regional economic and political integration, with a particular focus on southern Africa and the European Union. He is currently involved in a research project examining the impact on southern Africa of reforming the EU's sugar regime.

JEFFREY HERBST
Professor Jeffrey Herbst is Provost of Miami University of Ohio. Formerly he was Professor of Politics and International Affairs and Chair of the Department of Politics at Princeton University. His primary interests are in the politics of sub-Saharan Africa, the politics of political and economic reform, and the politics of boundaries. He is the author of *States and Power in Africa: Comparative Lessons in Authority and Control* (Princeton University

Press, 2000) and several other books and articles. He has also taught at the University of Zimbabwe, the University of Ghana, Legon, the University of Cape Town and the University of the Western Cape.

PARASCHAND HURRY
Praschand Hurry is the Senior Customs Affairs Officer, Trade, Customs and Monetary Affairs Division, COMESA and a Member, Panel of Fiscal Affairs, International Monetary Fund. As Senior Customs Officer in the Trade, Customs and Monetary Affairs Division at the COMESA Secretariat, he is responsible for co-ordinating trade and customs activities in the COMESA with particular focus on trade liberalization, rules of origin, trade remedies and Free Trade Area and some aspects of the customs modernization programme. He is presently involved in the preparatory work for the establishment of the COMESA Customs Union.

GREG MILLS
Dr Greg Mills is the Director of the Brenthurst Foundation based in Johannesburg, having served as the National Director of the South African Institute of International Affairs from 1996-2005. His book, *The Wired Model: South Africa, Foreign Policy and Globalisation*, was the winner of the Recht Malan Prize for the best non-fiction South African book in 2000. His other recent books include *Poverty to Prosperity: Globalisation, Good Governance and African Recovery, The Future of Africa: New Order in Sight?* (co-authored with Professor Jeffrey Herbst) and *The Security Intersection: The Paradox of Power in an Age of Terror*. Prior to joining SAIIA in 1994, he taught at the Universities of Cape Town and the Western Cape.

MONDE MUYANGWA
Dr Monde Muyangwa currently serves as Academic Dean at the Africa Center for Strategic Studies. In this capacity, she oversees all curriculum and programme development for the Africa Center's seminars and programmes, including Security Studies, Counter-Terrorism, Civil-Military Relations and Defense Economics. Dr Muyangwa possesses an extensive background in African development and US-Africa relations. Before joining the Africa Center, she worked as Director of Research and then Vice President for Research and Policy at the National Summit on Africa from 1997-2000. She has served as a development and gender consultant, and has worked on a wide range of community development projects in southern Africa in the areas of education, housing, health and nutrition. She has co-

authored, with Margaret Vogt, a publication for the International Peace Academy entitled *An Assessment of the Organization of African Unity's Mechanism for Conflict Prevention, Management and Resolution*.

SETH OBENG
Lieutenant General Seth Obeng is Army Chief of Staff, Ghana. He has held various military appointments including Commandant, Military Academy and Training School (MATS) and Ghana Armed Forces Command and Staff College (GAFCSC) as well as Chief of Staff, General Headquarters. He also served as Defence Advisor to the Ghana High Commission in London, 1984-1988. Lt Gen Obeng served as Deputy Force Commander for ECOMOG in Liberia, 1994-1996. He also served as Force Commander of the UN Observer and Monitoring Group (MONUA) in Angola, 1998-1999. He was then appointed Force Commander of the UN Interim Force in Lebanon (UNIFIL).

RAZEEN SALLY
Dr Razeen Sally is Senior Lecturer in International Political Economy at the London School of Economics, where he has taught since 1993 and is head of its International Trade Policy Unit. Dr Sally received his PhD from the LSE in 1992, having previously studied at the University of Frankfurt, the Free University of Berlin and the European University Institute in Florence, Italy. His research has focused on trade policies and policy-making in developing and transitional countries, and on developing country participation in the WTO. He has published *Classical Liberalism and International Economic Order: Studies in Theory and Intellectual History*. He has worked through Enterprise LSE, the Commonwealth Business Council and other national and international organizations on trade consultancy projects. He is on the Academic Advisory Council of the Institute of Economic Affairs in London, on the advisory board of the Cato Centre for Trade Policy Studies in Washington DC.

KURT SHILLINGER
Kurt Shillinger heads the Security and Terrorism in Africa research project at the South African Institute of International Affairs. He worked for *The Christian Science Monitor* for nine years from San Francisco, Boston and Washington, DC, holding such positions as Deputy Foreign Editor and Congressional Reporter. He covered the 1996 US presidential election as the Monitor's National Political Correspondent. In 1997, he moved to

South Africa as *The Boston Globe's Africa Correspondent*. He has reported from eighteen African countries and won the 2000 National Association of Black Journalists award for international reporting for his coverage of the HIV/AIDS epidemic.

MILLS SOKO

Dr Soko earned his BA in Social Sciences from the University of Cape Town in 1992. From 1994 to 1995 he was employed by the Institute for Democracy in South Africa as a researcher on parliamentary affairs, monitoring and preparing reports on parliamentary committees in South Africa's first democratic national legislature. In 1996, he joined the National Council of Provinces (NCOP) as a researcher to the Select Committee on Trade and Industry, Foreign Affairs and Public Enterprises. He was then appointed Director of Policy and Legislative Research at the NCOP. He resumed his studies and obtained an MA in International Political Economy from the University of Warwick, where he also completed a PhD on the political economy of trade policy reform in post-apartheid South Africa. He is currently a Director of Hluma Research and Business Services, and is a research associate of the South African Institute of International Affairs.

ANDREW STEWART

Major General Andrew Stewart was commissioned into the UK's 13th/18th Royal Hussars in 1972. In 1988 he was posted to SHAPE as MA to DSACEUR. He assumed command of The Light Dragoons in 1991, which he relinquished in 1993 to attend the Higher Command and Staff Course. He took command of 7th Armoured Brigade in 1996, spending April to October 1997 in Bosnia. 1999 saw him finishing command, attending RCDS and taking over as ACOS J3 at PJHQ where he oversaw UK operations in the Balkans, Middle East, Sierra Leone and Afghanistan. He moved to the Ministry of Defence and assumed the appointment of Director, Overseas Military Activity in 2001, which included strategic planning for Iraq, and established the Directorate of Strategic Planning. From Dec 2003 to July 2004 he deployed to Iraq as GOC MND(SE) in Basra. He assumed his present appointment as ACDS(Policy) in August 2004.